Farm Journal's
Homespun
Christmas

Farm Journal's Homespun Christmas

By the editors of Farm Journal

EDITOR: Nancy Steele

CRAFT EDITOR: Jean Gillies

FOOD EDITOR: Elise W. Manning

ASSOCIATE FOOD EDITOR: Patricia A. Ward

ASSISTANT EDITOR: Nancy Walker

CONTRIBUTING EDITORS: Janet Sanford
Claire McMullen

BOOK DESIGN: Maureen Sweeney

FARM JOURNAL, INC.
Philadelphia, Pennsylvania

Distributed to the trade by Doubleday & Company, Inc.
Garden City, New York

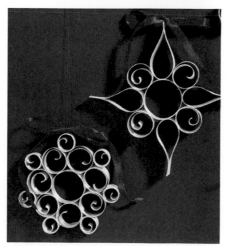

Christmas stockings from *Scrap Saver's Stitchery Book*,
Copyright © 1977, 1978 by Sandra Lounsbury Foose, Coun-
tryside Press, a division of Farm Journal, Inc., Philadelphia,
Pa., distributed to the trade by Doubleday & Company, Inc.,
Garden City, N.Y.

"Enjoying Christmas with Your Children" Copyright © 1977,
1978 by Channels to Children. From HOLIDAYS AND SEA-
SONS by Carol Beckman, Roberta Simmons and Nancy
Thomas. P.O. Box 7871, Colorado Springs, Colo. 80933.

Library of Congress Cataloging in Publication Data

Main entry under title: Farm journal's homespun Christmas.
  Includes index.
    1. Christmas cookery. 2. Christmas decorations.
I. Steele, Nancy Saunders. II. Farm journal (Philadelphia,
1956-   ) III. Title: Homespun Christmas.
TX739.F29   394.2'68282   79-12884

IBSN 0-89795-004-6

Contents

Introduction

Christmas in the Country 2
The Christmas Story 4

1 Family Feasting: The Foods We Remember

On Christmas Eve, Oyster Stew 6
A Christmas Dinner to Celebrate 8
It Wouldn't Be Christmas
  Without Cranberries 10
Lefse: A Tradition to Share 12

2 Holiday Dishes to Share

After Caroling, Stay for Supper 14
A Festive Buffet 16
Come for Coffee 18
Classic Ways with Cheese 21
Creative Cookies 24
The Sweetest of the Sweets 26
Breads and Jellies 28
Wrap-up: The Finishing Touch 31

3 O Christmas Tree!

From Seedling to Living Room
  /By Nancy Walker 34
Ornaments of Wood 38
Ornaments of Felt 41
Ornaments of Calico 47
Ornaments of Lace
  and Nostalgia 50

4 Deck the Halls

Threshold Greetings 53
Banners and Baskets 54
A Big Splash for a Small Space 58
Decorations for Dining 62
Cornhusk Craft 67
Clothespin Dolls 70

5 The Joy of Giving

Greetings to Make and Mail 72
The Gift That's Picture-Perfect 74
A Very Special Invitation
  /By Adelaide Altman 76
Accessories that Travel in Style 78
Applique for Tots and Teens 80
Double Cross-Stitch Pillows 82

6 Christmas is for Children

Long-legged Linda 84
Calico Critters 86
Childproof Decorations 88
Mouse House 90
Enjoying Christmas
  with Your Children
  /By Channels to Children 93
How to Become a Gift Detective 95

Appendix

How to Enlarge a Pattern 97
How to Transfer Pattern Details 97
How to Make
  Embroidery Stitches 98

Index

Index 123

Introduction
CHRISTMAS IN THE COUNTRY

Even those who have never known it, secretly yearn for it—an old-fashioned Christmas in the country, with fields of untrodden snow, tree branches draped as if in ermine, and a large, cheerful farmhouse to welcome everyone home.

Is Christmas in the country really what we imagine it to be? Come with us and see for yourself as we look in on farmhouses across America and share their ways of keeping the spirit of Christmas.

On a dairy farm in upstate New York, a woman is baking holiday breads and Christmas cookies, many of which will become gifts. "The extra energy that seems to flow at Christmas time is one of the things I like best about the season," she says. "It's the only time of year when I really feel like baking 20 dozen cookies!"

Such holiday baking is a big part of the Christmas celebration for most farm families—in fact, one grain farmer's wife in Michigan told us that she couldn't say just how much holiday baking she does, but added, "I used about 30 pounds of flour last year, if that gives you any idea." And a Nebraska livestock rancher says that no matter how much baking she does, it never seems to be enough: "The hardest part," she says, "is keeping the extra cooking and baking ahead of the extra eating!"

That's partly because Christmas in the country is a gathering of family and friends, whether it's a simple, quiet time of reflecting on the past year and counting blessings or a boisterous reunion of a clan of 35 or 40 family members.

A South Dakota farm woman sums it up nicely: "To me, Christmas is *family*. I want to do everything for everybody, give them all what they want, cook their favorite foods, invite friends in, just try to make everyone happy. Since this is impossible," she adds good-naturedly, "I just do the best I can."

Part of "doing the best" includes decorating, and beautiful homemade decorations abound in farmhouses during the Christmas season. An Illinois farm woman explains, "Christmas is one time of the year you can decorate your house and make all sorts of treats without an excuse!"

And of course, children make Christmas special; seeing their excitement as they open gifts is a joy. But to those who celebrate Christmas in the country, gift-giving is just as important as receiving.

A New Mexico farm woman smiles as she tells about a recent Christmas gift her daughter gave: a letter to her father promising to take out trash from the barn every day for a week. "Each year the gifts become less important and the people become more important," agrees a woman on a livestock and grain farm in Colorado.

This loving and giving spirit reflects what Christmas really means—a chance for each family to stop and celebrate the birth of Christ in their own way. In many homes, the Christmas story is read aloud each year on Christmas Eve, and church bells peal through the night air as farm families all over the country attend Christmas Eve services. In many communities, the children participate in a living Nativity scene on the church lawn.

In New Jersey, a farm family works together to fill stockings and food boxes for needy families. A Texas family brings the Christmas message to neighbors and friends by caroling from ranch to ranch on horseback. And an Idaho family's favorite Christmas took place one year when the lake froze: "We took wieners and marshmallows, built a fire and made hot chocolate. We ice skated until the moon came up and the stars were reflected in the ice. Absolutely spectacular!"

Christmas in the country? It's different each year, in every home.

A Montana teen says: "Christmas in my home means a super-smelling juniper tree with curvature of the spine! It also means getting small luxuries rather than large necessities, making Christmas cookies after Christmas, and sharing secrets with a temporarily angelic brother."

In the country, as all over the world, families have their own ways of making this the happiest time of the year. May it be so at your home, and for all the Christmases to come.

The
Christmas Story

For directions on how to make this crewel work, see p. 99.

*A*nd it came to pass in those days, that there went out a decree from Caesar Augustus, that all the world should be taxed. ☐ (And this taxing was first made when Cyrenius was governor of Syria.) ☐ And all went to be taxed, every one into his own city. ☐ And Joseph also went up from Galilee, out of the city of Nazareth, into Judea, unto the city of David, which is called Bethlehem; (because he was of the house and lineage of David:) ☐ To be taxed with Mary his espoused wife, being great with child. ☐ And so it was, that, while they were there, the days were accomplished that she should be delivered. ☐ And she brought forth her firstborn son, and wrapped him in swaddling clothes, and laid him in a manger; because there was no room for them in the inn. ☐ And there were in the same country shepherds abiding in the field, keeping watch over their flock by night. ☐ And, lo, the angel of the Lord came upon them, and the glory of the Lord shone round about them: and they were sore afraid. ☐ And the angel said unto them, Fear not: for, behold, I bring you good tidings of great joy, which shall be to all people. ☐ For unto you is born this day in the city of David a Saviour, which is Christ the Lord. ☐ And this shall be a sign unto you; Ye shall find the babe wrapped in swaddling clothes, lying in a manger. ☐ And suddenly there was with the angel a multitude of the heavenly host praising God, and saying, ☐ Glory to God in the highest, and on earth peace, good will toward men.

Luke 2: 1-14

CHAPTER 1

FAMILY FEASTING: THE FOODS WE REMEMBER

Reminiscences of past Christmases always seem to turn to food, for holiday dining rituals are among the most important in our lives. And when it comes to Christmas Eve suppers and Christmas dinner with all the trimmings, each family has its own traditions.

We asked farm families across the country to share with us some of the food traditions that make Christmas so special. They talked about Christmas Eve with oyster stew, all hot and steaming and buttery. And about lefse, a Norwegian bread whose taste has carried its popularity to other farm homes. And finally, about cranberries, served dozens of ways at the big traditional meal.

On the pages that follow we offer a sampling of traditional foods served on Christmas Eve and Christmas Day, as well as some new recipes to help you keep Christmas in your own way.

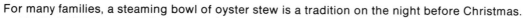

For many families, a steaming bowl of oyster stew is a tradition on the night before Christmas.

On Christmas Eve, Oyster Stew

Christmas Eve is perhaps the most magical night of the year: The sights, sounds and smells of Christmas are everywhere. Many families attend candlelight church services, exchange Christmas gifts and share a traditional Christmas Eve supper.

In many farm and ranch homes across the country, oyster stew has been the favored Christmas Eve supper ever since refrigerated railroad cars began to chug out of the East toward the Midwest.

A retired rancher remembers going to the butcher shop with his dad back in 1904 to buy fresh oysters for stew. "They came in square tin cans with large openings in the top that were snugly sealed with a big cork. They were big, fat oysters with lots of liquid and tasted so good," he recalls, "and they were very inexpensive in those days, so we enjoyed them often."

Today, farm women may vary their own versions of oyster stew each year according to the number of oysters the budget allows. In addition, some cooks have very definite feelings about oyster stew: It must have cream, or evaporated milk, or be slightly thickened with flour or cornstarch.

We share three heirloom oyster stew recipes with you. When poured steaming hot over pats of butter in individual serving bowls, each version provides a meal light enough to serve youngsters on the eve of a day filled with excitement.

OYSTER STEW I

Light cream produces a rich stew—there's no thickening in this extra-creamy version.

1 qt. milk
1 c. light cream
1 tsp. salt
⅛ tsp. pepper
½ c. butter or regular margarine
2 pt. shucked stewing oysters in own liquor

Combine milk, cream, salt and pepper in 4-qt. Dutch oven. Heat over medium heat until scalded. Meanwhile, melt butter in 2-qt. saucepan over low heat.

Add oysters with liquor. Cook just a few minutes or until oysters begin to curl around the edges. Pour oyster mixture into hot milk. Heat and serve immediately. Makes about 2 quarts or 8 (1-cup) servings.

OYSTER STEW II

Made with milk and thickened with flour, this version is popular with folks who like oyster stew with a little body.

3 qt. milk
4 tblsp. flour
3 tsp. salt
¼ tsp. pepper
¼ c. water
2 pt. shucked stewing oysters in own liquor
3 tblsp. butter or regular margarine

Pour milk into 5-qt. Dutch oven. Heat over medium heat until scalded. Meanwhile, combine flour, salt, pepper and water in small jar. Cover and shake until blended.

Pour oysters with liquor in 3-qt. saucepan. Slowly stir in flour mixture. Cook just a few minutes over low heat, stirring constantly, until mixture thickens and oysters begin to curl around the edges. Pour oyster mixture into hot milk. Add butter. Heat and serve immediately. Makes about 4 quarts or 16 (1-cup) servings.

OYSTER STEW III

If you're one of those cooks who prefer fewer oysters and more milk, try this version.

2 qt. milk
2 tblsp. flour
1 tsp. salt
¹/₁₆ tsp. pepper
¼ c. water
½ pt. shucked stewing oysters in own liquor
butter or regular margarine

Pour milk into 4-qt. Dutch oven. Heat over medium heat until scalded. Meanwhile, combine flour, salt, pepper and water in small jar. Cover and shake until blended.

Pour oysters with liquor into 2-qt. saucepan. Slowly stir in flour mixture. Cook over low heat, stirring constantly, until mixture thickens and oysters begin to curl around the edges. Pour oyster mixture into hot milk. Cover and remove from heat. Let stand 15 minutes. Serve in bowls over pats of butter. Makes about 2 quarts or 8 (1-cup) servings.

A Christmas Dinner to Celebrate

Christmas is the one day of the year when everyone tries to be home for the holidays. But the person who has the least time to visit with the family is the hostess—she's busy in the kitchen stuffing the turkey and mashing the potatoes.

Our solution was to develop a recipe for Creamy Mashed Potatoes that can be made the day before. Then we created a super-speedy dressing to banish the chore of stuffing the turkey. Range Top Pecan Dressing is our homemade country version of the commercial stuffing that cooks quickly on top of the stove: you can make the bread crumbs weeks in advance and assemble the rest of the ingredients the day before the big feast. On Christmas Day, just heat the potatoes and prepare the dressing—it cooks in just 15 minutes. Then relax and enjoy the extra time with your family.

CHRISTMAS DINNER

Chilled Citrus Cup
Roast Turkey
Range Top Pecan Dressing★
Creamy Mashed Potatoes★
Butternut Squash With Peas★
Golden Parmesan Rolls★
Cranberry Blender Relish★
Hot Mince Pie
Pumpkin Pie
Coffee, Tea

★ *Recipes follow*

CREAMY MASHED POTATOES

5 lb. all-purpose potatoes, pared and quartered
2 tsp. salt
2 (3-oz.) pkg. cream cheese with chives, cubed
4 tblsp. butter or regular margarine
½ tsp. garlic salt
¼ tsp. pepper
2 c. heavy cream
2 tblsp. butter or regular margarine
paprika

Cook potatoes with 1 tsp. of the salt in boiling water in Dutch oven until tender, about 30 minutes. Drain well.

Mash potatoes with potato masher until smooth. Add cream cheese, 4 tblsp. butter, garlic salt, pepper and remaining 1 tsp. salt. Mix until smooth. Gradually add heavy cream, mixing until smooth after each addition. Turn the potato mixture into greased 13x9x2-inch (3-qt.) baking dish. (Bake at once or cover with foil; refrigerate overnight.)

Dot top of potatoes with remaining 2 tblsp. butter and sprinkle with paprika. Bake in 325° oven 30 minutes. Increase heat to 375° and bake 30 minutes more or until hot. Makes 12 servings.

RANGE TOP PECAN DRESSING

8 c. white bread cubes (⅜-inch)
2 c. celery slices (⅛-inch)
1 c. chopped onion
¼ c. chopped fresh parsley
½ c. butter or regular margarine
1 (4-oz.) can sliced mushrooms
1 (13¾-oz.) can chicken broth
2 tsp. rubbed sage
⅛ tsp. pepper
1 c. pecan halves

Advance preparation: Toast half of bread cubes by spreading in a single layer in a 15½x10½x1-inch jelly roll pan. Bake in 325° oven, stirring frequently, until dry and golden brown, about 15 minutes. Repeat with remaining bread cubes. May be stored in plastic bag or airtight container up to 6 weeks.

The Day before: Cut celery, onion and parsley. Place on plate; cover with plastic wrap. Refrigerate overnight.

Christmas Day: Melt butter in Dutch oven. Add celery and onion; saute until tender, about 10 minutes. Add parsley; cook 2 more minutes. Drain mushrooms, reserving liquid. Add enough water to liquid to make ⅔ c. Add mushrooms, ⅔ c. reserved liquid, chicken broth, sage and pepper to Dutch oven. Cover and simmer 5 minutes.

Remove from heat. Stir in toasted bread cubes and pe-

Surrounding the turkey, clockwise from left, are Creamy Mashed Potatoes, Golden Parmesan Rolls, Butternut Squash with Peas, Cranberry Blender Relish and Range Top Pecan Dressing. (For cranberry recipe, see p. 11.)

cans. Cover and let stand 10 minutes. Makes 6 to 8 servings.

BUTTERNUT SQUASH WITH PEAS

3 (1½-lb.) butternut squash (4½ lb.)
1 tsp. salt
2 (10-oz.) pkg. frozen peas (4 c.)
6 tblsp. butter or regular margarine

Pare the squash and remove seeds. Cut in 1-inch chunks. Bring 1 inch of water and 1 tsp. salt in Dutch oven to a boil. Add squash and cook, covered, 10 minutes.

Add peas. Cook, covered, 5 to 7 minutes more or until vege-tables are tender. Drain well. Add butter. Makes 12 servings.

GOLDEN PARMESAN ROLLS

2 pkg. active dry yeast
3¼ c. sifted flour
½ c. milk
½ c. water
½ c. butter or regular margarine
¼ c. sugar
2 tsp. salt
1 egg
1 c. grated Parmesan cheese
1 egg yolk, slightly beaten
1 tsp. water
sesame seeds

Stir yeast and 1 c. of the flour into mixing bowl.

Heat together milk, ½ c. water, butter, sugar and salt in sauce-pan to very warm (120-130°F). Add hot liquid to flour-yeast mix-ture. Beat with electric mixer at medium speed 3 minutes or until smooth. Blend in egg, Parmesan and 1 c. more of the flour. Beat 2 more minutes. Stir in remaining flour to make a stiff batter. Cov-er; let rise in warm place until doubled, about an hour.

Divide dough in fourths. With greased hands, shape each fourth into 9 balls. Place balls in-to greased, 3-inch muffin-pan cups, 3 balls in each cup. Brush tops with combined egg yolk and 1 tsp. water. Sprinkle with sesame seeds. Cover and let rise until almost doubled, about 30 minutes.

Bake in 325° oven 30 minutes or until golden brown. Makes 12.

9

Here are four ways to add color and sparkle to your holiday table: Cranberry-Orange Ring, Cranberry Blender Relish, Cranberry-Marshmallow Cream, and a Two-Layer Cranberry-Cream Cheese Mold topped with maraschino cherries.

It Wouldn't Be Christmas Without Cranberries

Nothing adds sparkle to a holiday table quite like the bright crimson of cranberries, whether served as a sauce, in a mold or as a tart relish.

Here are the special cranberry creations of four country cooks—each recipe a superb addition to any holiday menu.

10

CRANBERRY BLENDER RELISH

1 env. unflavored gelatin
1 c. cold water
2 c. cranberries
  (fresh or frozen)
1 medium navel orange, seeded
  and cut in eighths
1 medium apple, cored and cut
  in eighths
¾ c. sugar
¼ c. chopped walnuts

Soften gelatin in cold water in saucepan 5 minutes.

Warm over low heat until gelatin is dissolved. Place cranberries, orange, apple, sugar and gelatin mixture in blender. Cover and blend until orange peel is finely chopped. Fold in walnuts. Pour into serving bowl. Cover and refrigerate until well chilled. Garnish with halved orange slices, if you wish. Makes about 4 cups.

CRANBERRY-ORANGE RING

1 medium navel orange, seeded
  and quartered
2 c. cranberries
  (fresh or frozen)
½ c. sugar
¼ c. light corn syrup
2 (3-oz.) pkg. lemon-flavored
  gelatin
1½ c. boiling water
½ c. cold water
Whipped Dressing (recipe
  follows)

Grind orange with peel, using coarse blade of food grinder. (Orange mixture, including juice, should measure ¾ c.)

Grind orange again with cranberries, using coarse blade of food grinder. Add sugar and corn syrup; set aside.

Dissolve gelatin in boiling water in bowl. Stir in cold water. Chill until thick and syrupy. Fold in cranberry-orange mixture. Pour into 5-c. ring mold. Chill until set.

Unmold gelatin on plate. Fill center of ring with Whipped Dressing. Makes 10 servings.

Whipped Dressing

1 (2-oz.) env. whipped topping
  mix
½ c. cold milk
½ tsp. vanilla
½ c. salad dressing or
  mayonnaise
1 tblsp. milk

Combine topping mix, cold milk and vanilla in shallow mixing bowl. Beat with electric mixer at high speed until soft peaks form. In another bowl, blend salad dressing or mayonnaise with 1 tblsp. milk. Fold into whipped topping. Makes about 1½ cups.

CRANBERRY-MARSHMALLOW CREAM

1 lb. ground cranberries
  (fresh or frozen)
1 (20-oz.) can crushed
  pineapple, drained
1 c. sugar
1 (10½-oz.) bag miniature
  marshmallows
2 c. heavy cream, whipped

Mix together cranberries, pineapple and sugar in bowl.

Fold marshmallows into the whipped cream. Fold cranberry mixture into whipped cream mixture. Chill until serving time. To prepare recipe a day or two in advance, chill cream and cranberry mixture separately, and fold together just before serving. Makes 10 cups or 20 (½-cup) servings.

TWO-LAYER CRANBERRY-CREAM CHEESE MOLD

1 (3-oz.) pkg. cream cheese,
  softened
1 c. heavy cream
16 large marshmallows,
  quartered
1 lb. cranberries
  (fresh or frozen)
1 medium apple, cored and
  quartered
1 c. sugar
2 (3-oz.) pkg. cherry-flavored
  gelatin
2 c. boiling water
½ c. chopped walnuts
8 red and 8 green candied or
  maraschino cherries

Whip cream cheese in bowl until creamy, using electric mixer. At low speed, gradually add heavy cream (do not beat). Stir in marshmallows. Cover and chill overnight to soften marshmallows.

Grind together cranberries and apple in food grinder, using coarse blade. Add sugar; set aside.

Dissolve gelatin in boiling water in bowl. Chill until thick and syrupy. Fold in cranberry mixture and walnuts. Pour into 12x 8x2-inch glass baking dish (2-qt.). Cover; chill until set.

Whip chilled marshmallow topping at high speed until thick and creamy, using electric mixer. Spread over gelatin. Chill until serving time. To garnish, cut 8 red cherries in half. Space halves evenly on top of cream layer. Cut green cherries into pieces resembling stems and leaves. Arrange next to red cherry halves to form flowers (see photo). Makes 16 servings.

11

Lefse: A Tradition to Share

If you could peek through the kitchen windows of farm houses on any "baking day" in December, you'd probably see mothers and children baking dozens and dozens of cookies. And on Norwegian-American farms, chances are you'd see women rolling out large tissue-thin circles of lefse.

Lefse is a simple bread that's baked on a griddle and served at meals throughout the Christmas season. It's always served cold. Some like it plain, spread lavishly with softened butter, while others

sprinkle brown sugar over the butter and fold the lefse into fourths or roll into a cylinder.

Many farm women don't even use a recipe for lefse. They make it just like their mothers did—"by touch and feel." Whether you follow a recipe or use your instincts, lefse should be "as soft as a baby's cheek," a Wisconsin farm woman told us. Even if you aren't Norwegian, you might like to make lefse part of your holiday meals. Here are three versions of this classic dish.

LEFSE I

A little half-and-half added to the dough makes this lefse just a wee bit richer.

2 lb. baking potatoes (4 large), pared and quartered
1 tsp. salt

¼ c. butter or regular margarine, melted
¼ c. half-and-half
2¼ c. sifted flour

Cook potatoes with salt in boiling water in saucepan until tender. Drain well. Rice potatoes, using a potato ricer. Cover

and chill in refrigerator 8 hours or overnight.

Firmly pack chilled, riced potatoes into measuring cup. (You will need 3½ c.) Return to bowl. Add melted butter and half-and-half, mixing with a large spoon until smooth.

Mix in flour, a little at a time,

until dough forms. Shape mixture into 12-inch roll. (Be sure to remove all air from mixture when shaping into roll.) Divide roll into 12 pieces.

Roll out each piece of dough very thinly on well-floured pastry cloth to 12-inch circle, using stockinet-covered rolling pin. The lefse should be very thin, about $1/16$-inch thick. Carefully roll lefse around rolling pin so it can be transferred to griddle.

To bake: Bake lefse, one at a time, on ungreased very hot griddle or in 12-inch skillet (475°). (Test temperature by sprinkling a little flour on the griddle; if it browns immediately, the temperature is right.) When small brown spots appear on the underside of the lefse, turn over, using a long metal spatula. When browned on both sides, fold into fourths, using metal spatula. Remove from griddle. Place immediately on a dish towel (do not use terry towels) and cover with another towel. This is important in order to hold in the steam and keep the lefse moist.

Bake another lefse and place on top of the first one, placing the point of the wedge in the opposite direction so that lefse will stack evenly. Re-cover with towel. Continue in this way until all lefse are prepared. Cool to room temperature.

When lefse are cool, remove from towels. Wrap in plastic wrap, placing 6 in each package. Store wrapped packages in plastic bags to keep lefse soft. They can be stored up to 5 days in the refrigerator. Makes 12 lefse.

To serve: Lefse should always be served at room temperature. Unfold lefse and cut in half. Spread with softened butter and sprinkle with brown or white sugar. Fold each half into thirds, forming pie-shaped wedges.

LEFSE II

Baking powder makes this lefse slightly puffier than others.

2 lb. baking potatoes (4 large), pared and quartered
½ c. soft butter or regular margarine
1¾ c. sifted flour
1 tblsp. sugar
1 tsp. salt
½ tsp. baking powder

Cook potatoes in boiling water in saucepan until tender. Drain well. Rice potatoes, using a potato ricer. Stir with fork until the mixture is smooth. Pack hot mashed potatoes into measuring cup. (You will need 3 c.) Add butter to hot potatoes. Cool mixture slightly. Cover and chill in refrigerator 8 hours or overnight.

Sift together flour, sugar, salt and baking powder. Add flour mixture to potatoes, a little at a time, until dough forms.

Shape mixture into 12-inch roll. (Be sure to remove all air from mixture when shaping roll.) Divide roll into 12 pieces.

Roll out each piece of dough very thinly on well-floured pastry cloth to 10-inch circle, using stockinet-covered rolling pin. The lefse should be very thin, about $1/16$-inch thick. Carefully roll lefse around rolling pin so it can be transferred to griddle.

To bake: See directions for Lefse I.

When lefse are cooled, remove from towels. Wrap, still folded, in plastic wrap, placing 6 in a package. Store wrapped packages in plastic bags to keep lefse soft. They can be stored up to 5 days in the refrigerator. Makes 12 lefse.

To serve: See directions for Lefse I.

LEFSE III

Shortening is substituted for some of the butter in this traditional version of lefse.

2 lb. baking potatoes (4 large), pared and quartered
¼ c. butter or regular margarine
2 c. sifted flour
1½ tsp. sugar
½ tsp. salt
2 tblsp. melted shortening

Cook potatoes in boiling water in saucepan until tender. Drain well. Rice potatoes, using a potato ricer. Stir with fork until mixture is smooth. Pack hot potatoes into measuring cup. (You will need 3 c.) Add butter to hot potatoes. Cool mixture to room temperature.

Sift together flour, sugar and salt. Stir melted shortening into potatoes. Add flour mixture, a little at a time, until dough forms.

Shape mixture into 14-inch roll. (Be sure to remove all air from mixture when shaping roll.) Divide roll into 14 pieces.

Roll out each piece of dough very thinly on well-floured pastry cloth to 9-inch circle, using stockinet-covered rolling pin. The lefse should be very thin, about $1/16$-inch thick. Carefully roll lefse around rolling pin so it can be transferred to griddle.

To bake: See directions for Lefse I.

When lefse are cool, remove from towels. Wrap, still folded, in plastic wrap, placing 7 in a package. Store wrapped packages in plastic bags to keep lefse soft. They can be stored up to 5 days in the refrigerator. Makes 14 lefse.

To serve: Lefse should always be served at room temperature. Unfold lefse. Spread with softened butter and sprinkle with brown or white sugar. Roll up to form a cylinder.

CHAPTER 2

HOLIDAY DISHES TO SHARE

Christmas is a time for sharing—the comforts of your home, the warmth of your companionship and the bounty of the land. A homemade treat from the kitchen is a gift that's guaranteed to fit the recipient, and it's one of the warmest holiday greetings you can send, whether it's shared as part of the hospitality of your home or delivered with a sprig of holly and a kiss.

In this chapter you'll find recipes for holiday cookies, breads, jellies and candies, with instructions for creative ways to package them. And because hospitality is such a big part of Christmas, we've included ideas for informal entertaining.

After Caroling, Stay for Supper

It's the season for impromptu invitations: Stop by to see our tree and have some eggnog . . . come for caroling and stay for supper.

For unexpected company, stock the refrigerator with a pitcher of frothy eggnog—a healthful version laced with orange juice and made with a whipped topping mix to cut both cost and calories.

To welcome a group of carolers in from the most wintry of December nights, plan a dinner around Meatball and Bean Stew. It can be made the day before and reheated while you join the festivities. Set out a platter of Creamy Tuna Spread and crackers as an appetizer, then let your friends help themselves to a supper of stew, Mixed-Vegetable Marinade and hot rolls. For an elegant finale, serve individual cheesecakes. These can be made a month in advance and frozen. An assortment of these packed in a pretty tin also makes a handsome gift.

CREAMY TUNA SPREAD

6 hard-cooked eggs, sliced
2 (8-oz.) pkg. cream cheese
2 (7-oz.) cans tuna, drained and
    flaked
¼ c. minced green onions and
    tops
2 tblsp. minced fresh parsley
2 tsp. Worcestershire sauce
2 tsp. lemon juice
½ tsp. salt
chopped fresh parsley

Reserve 8 center egg slices for garnish. Chop remaining egg. Blend cream cheese until softened. Add chopped egg, tuna, green onions, 2 tblsp. parsley, Worcestershire sauce, lemon juice and salt. Mix until blended. Chill at least 2 hours.

Divide mixture in half. Shape into 2 balls. Roll each in parsley. Garnish bottom edge with egg slices cut in half. Makes 4 cups.

MIXED-VEGETABLE MARINADE

1 medium cauliflower, cut up
4 medium carrots, pared and
    cut in 2-inch strips
1 (1-lb.) can wax beans, drained
1 (1-lb.) can whole green beans,
    drained
1 c. sliced celery
1 medium onion, sliced
1 (8-oz.) bottle regular Italian
    salad dressing
12 medium ripe olives, pitted

Cook cauliflower and carrots in boiling salted water in Dutch oven for 5 minutes or until tender-crisp. Drain. Plunge into ice water; drain well. Combine cooled vegetables with remaining ingredients in bowl. Toss gently to mix. Cover; refrigerate overnight. Can be stored up to 5 days. Makes 10 servings.

FLUFFY ORANGE NOG

2 env. whipped topping mix
6 eggs, separated
pinch of salt
3 tblsp. sugar
2 tsp. grated orange rind
1 c. heavy cream
2 c. milk
4 c. orange juice
6 tblsp. sugar
ground nutmeg

Prepare topping mix according to directions on package.

Combine egg yolks, salt, 3 tblsp. sugar and orange rind in large bowl. Beat until lemon-colored, about 5 minutes. Beat in heavy cream and milk. Slowly stir in orange juice. Fold some of yolk mixture into whipped topping. Then fold whipped topping back into egg yolk mixture.

Beat egg whites until frothy. Gradually beat in 6 tblsp. sugar. Fold egg yolk mixture into egg whites. Refrigerate. Stir well before serving; sprinkle with nutmeg. Can be stored up to 3 days. Makes about a gallon.

MINIATURE CHEESECAKE JEWELS

3 (8-oz.) pkg. cream cheese
1 c. sugar
¼ tsp. salt
1 tsp. vanilla
5 eggs
1 pt. dairy sour cream
assorted canned fruits, cut into small pieces
walnut halves or sliced almonds

Beat cream cheese at medium speed of electric mixer until smooth. Gradually beat in sugar. Blend in salt and vanilla. Add eggs one at a time, beating well after each addition. Spoon into paper-lined 1¼-inch muffin-pan cups, filling almost full.

Bake in 325° oven 30 minutes or until set. Cool in pans 5 minutes. Remove. When cool, cover and refrigerate. Can be stored up to 5 days. The day before you plan to serve them, swirl each cheesecake with sour cream. Decorate with fruits and nuts. Cover and refrigerate. Makes 60.
To freeze: Undecorated cheesecakes can be frozen as long as four weeks.

MEATBALL AND BEAN STEW

1 lb. ground beef
½ c. fresh bread crumbs
¼ c. minced onion
3 tblsp. minced fresh parsley
1 tsp. salt
½ tsp. oregano leaves
¼ tsp. basil leaves
1 egg
¼ c. milk
2 tblsp. cooking oil
1 c. green pepper strips (1-inch)
2 (1-lb. 1-oz.) cans kidney beans
1 (1-lb. 12-oz.) can Italian tomatoes, cut up
1 (15-oz.) can tomato sauce
1 bay leaf
½ tsp. oregano leaves
½ tsp. basil leaves
shredded Cheddar cheese

Combine ground beef, bread crumbs, onion, parsley, salt, ½ tsp. oregano, ¼ tsp. basil, egg and milk in bowl. Mix lightly, but well. Shape into 32 meatballs. Brown in hot oil in Dutch oven; remove as they brown. Pour off all but 2 tblsp. fat.

Saute green pepper in fat until tender. Add remaining ingredients except cheese; mix well. Add meatballs. Simmer uncovered 30 minutes. If you like, pour into 13x9x2-inch (3-qt.) serving dish. Top with cheese and serve in bowls. Makes 10 servings.

A Festive Buffet

Baked ham is a popular party dish because it can be cooked several days in advance and served cold. But what to serve with it?

Pictured here are the makings of a buffet that can be prepared the day before. Building on your own version of baked ham, we've added a Shimmering Apple Mold, Au Gratin Potato Bake and a Holiday Trifle flavored with raspberries and almonds. Only the trifle needs last-minute attention.

SHIMMERING APPLE MOLD

1 (8½-oz.) can crushed pine-
    apple
½ c. sugar
⅛ tsp. salt
3 tblsp. lemon juice
2 eggs, beaten
1 c. heavy cream, whipped
2 c. diced, unpared apples
1½ c. miniature marshmallows
½ c. finely chopped celery

Drain pineapple, reserving juice. Add enough water to juice to make ½ c.

Combine sugar, salt and lemon juice in a small saucepan. Gradually stir in reserved ½ c. liquid and eggs. Cook over low heat, stirring constantly, until thickened. Cool completely.

Fold in whipped cream, apples, marshmallows, celery and pineapple. Pour into lightly oiled 9x5x3-inch loaf pan. Cover with foil and freeze.

To unmold, invert on serving plate and remove loaf pan. Garnish with chicory and whole fresh cranberries, if you wish. Makes 8 servings.

AU GRATIN POTATO BAKE

4 lb. unpared potatoes, cooked
    and drained
1½ c. shredded Cheddar
    cheese
1 c. chopped onion
¼ c. butter or regular margarine
1 (10¾-oz.) can condensed
    cream of celery soup
1 pt. dairy sour cream
½ c. crushed cornflakes
3 tblsp. melted butter or regular
    margarine
pimiento strips
chopped fresh parsley

Remove skins from potatoes. Shred potatoes into bowl, using medium blade of shredder. Add cheese.

Saute onion in ¼ c. melted butter in saucepan until tender. Remove from heat. Stir in soup and sour cream. Pour over potatoes and cheese; mix well. Turn into greased 13x9x2-inch (3 qt.) baking dish. Cover; refrigerate overnight.

Sprinkle with cornflakes; drizzle with 3 tblsp. butter.

Bake in 350° oven 1 hour. Garnish with pimiento and parsley. Makes 12 servings.

HOLIDAY TRIFLE

5 eggs
¾ c. sugar
½ tsp. almond flavoring
¾ c. sifted cake flour
¾ tsp. baking powder
¼ tsp. salt
Raspberry Sauce (recipe
    follows)
Custard Sauce (recipe follows)
1 (1-lb. 13-oz.) can sliced
    peaches, well drained
1⅓ c. flaked coconut
1 pt. heavy cream
¼ c. sugar
1 tsp. vanilla
toasted slivered almonds
red maraschino cherries

Combine eggs, ¾ c. sugar and almond flavoring in mixing bowl. Beat until thick and lemon-colored, using electric mixer at high speed.

Sift together cake flour, baking powder and salt. Fold into egg mixture. Turn into a well-greased 15½x10½x1-inch jelly roll pan.

Bake in 350° oven 20 minutes or until done. Turn out on rack to cool.

Prepare Raspberry Sauce and Custard Sauce.

Divide cake into thirds. Tear each third into small pieces.

Layer one third of cake into 4-qt. crystal bowl. Top with one third of Raspberry Sauce, one third of Custard Sauce, one half of peaches and one half of coconut. Repeat layers. Top with the remaining cake, Raspberry Sauce and Custard Sauce. Refrigerate at least 1 hour.

Whip cream together with ¼ c. sugar and vanilla until thick and creamy. Swirl over dessert; decorate with almonds and cherries. Makes 12 servings.

Raspberry Sauce: Drain 2 (10-oz.) pkg. frozen raspberries, thawed, reserving juice. Add enough water to juice to make 1½ c. Combine ¼ c. sugar and 2 tblsp. cornstarch in 2-qt. saucepan. Gradually stir in 1½ c. liquid and 1 tblsp. lemon juice. Cook, stirring constantly, until thickened.

Remove from heat. Add raspberries and cool well.

Custard Sauce: Prepare 1 (4¾-oz.) pkg. vanilla pudding and pie filling with 3¾ c. milk according to package directions. Cool to room temperature. Stir in 1½ tsp. vanilla.

Come for Coffee

In the country, an invitation to "come for coffee" promises a special treat: perhaps a buttery brioche; perhaps a taste of Finnish Braid drizzled with almond glaze; or maybe—just maybe—a tall slice of Christmas Coffee Ring filled with walnuts and honey and studded with cherries.

Here are five holiday breads to serve on special occasions, to send as gifts, or just to enjoy with a cup of coffee around the kitchen table.

FINNISH COFFEE BRAID

2 c. milk
1 c. sugar
¼ c. butter or regular margarine
1 tsp. salt
2 pkg. active dry yeast
½ c. lukewarm water (110°)
2 eggs
1 tsp. crushed cardamom seeds
8½ to 9 c. sifted flour
Almond Glaze (recipe follows)
silver dragees
red and green candied cherries

Scald milk. Pour over sugar, butter and salt in mixing bowl. Cool to lukewarm.

Sprinkle yeast on lukewarm water and stir to dissolve. Add yeast, eggs, cardamom seeds and 2 c. of the flour to milk mixture. Beat with electric mixer at medium speed until smooth, about 2 minutes, scraping bowl occasionally. (Or beat with a spoon until batter is smooth.)

Gradually add enough remaining flour, a little at a time, to make a soft dough that leaves the sides of the bowl. Turn onto a lightly floured surface and knead until smooth and satiny, about 8 to 10 minutes.

Place in a lightly greased bowl, turning dough over once to grease the top. Cover and let rise in a warm place until doubled, about 1 to 1½ hours.

Divide dough into 4 portions. Divide each portion into thirds. Roll each into a 10-inch strip. Braid 3 strips together. Repeat to make four loaves. Place on 2 greased baking sheets. Let rise until doubled.

Bake in 375° oven 20 to 25 minutes or until golden brown. Remove from baking sheets and cool on racks. While warm, drizzle with Almond Glaze. Decorate with silver dragees, red candied cherries and leaves cut from green candied cherries. Makes 4 loaves.

Almond Glaze: Combine 2 c. sifted confectioners sugar, 3 tblsp. milk and ½ tsp. almond flavoring in bowl. Blend until smooth.

CHRISTMAS EVE SAFFRON BRAID

1 c. milk, scalded
½ c. sugar
2 tblsp. butter or regular margarine
½ tsp. salt
¹/₁₆ tsp. powdered saffron
1 pkg. active dry yeast
¼ c. lukewarm water (110°)
1 egg
½ tsp. ground cardamom
4¼ c. sifted flour
Icing (recipe follows)
candied red and green cherries
toasted slivered almonds

Pour milk over sugar, butter, salt and saffron in mixing bowl. Cool to lukewarm.

Dissolve yeast in lukewarm water. Add yeast, egg, cardamom and 1 c. of the flour to milk mixture. Beat with electric mixer at medium speed until smooth, about 2 minutes. Gradually stir in enough remaining flour to make a soft dough. Knead on floured surface until smooth and satiny, about 5 minutes.

Place in lightly greased bowl, turning dough over once to grease top. Cover and let rise in warm place until doubled, about 1½ hours.

Divide dough in thirds. Shape each into a 21-inch strip. Place on greased baking sheet. Braid three strips together; pinch ends to seal. Cover; let rise until doubled, 1 to 1¼ hours.

Bake in 350° oven 25 minutes or until golden brown. Remove from baking sheet; cool on rack. Drizzle with Icing. Decorate with

(continued on p. 20)

Above, from left: Regal Savarin Ring, Christmas Morning
Brioche and Christmas Eve Saffron Braid

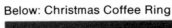
Below: Christmas Coffee Ring

Below: Finnish Coffee Braid

cherries and almonds. Makes 1 loaf.

Icing: Combine 1 c. sifted confectioners sugar, 1 tblsp. milk and ½ tsp. vanilla in bowl; beat until smooth.

CHRISTMAS MORNING BRIOCHE

¼ c. milk
1 c. butter or regular margarine
½ c. sugar
½ tsp. salt
2 tsp. grated lemon rind
2 pkg. active dry yeast
¼ c. lukewarm water (110°)
6 eggs
4½ c. sifted flour
1 egg white, slightly beaten
1 tblsp. water

Heat milk and butter over low heat in saucepan until butter is melted. Pour over sugar, salt and lemon rind in bowl; cool to lukewarm. Dissolve yeast in ¼ c. lukewarm water. Add yeast and eggs to milk mixture; blend well. Add 3 c. of the flour; beat with electric mixer at medium speed 4 minutes. Stir in remaining flour; beat until smooth. Cover; let rise in warm place until doubled, 1 to 1¼ hours. Stir down dough. Cover with foil. Refrigerate overnight.

Divide dough in 32 pieces. With floured hands, shape 24 pieces into balls. Place in greased 3-inch fluted brioche pans or muffin-pan cups. Flatten and make an indentation in center of each. Divide each remaining piece into 3 parts. Shape into 24 teardrop shapes. Place in indentations pointed-side down. Let rise until doubled, about 45 minutes. Brush with combined egg white and 1 tblsp. water.

Bake in 375° oven 12 to 15 minutes or until golden brown. Makes 24.

REGAL SAVARIN RING

1 pkg. active dry yeast
⅓ c. lukewarm water (110°)
½ c. sifted flour
1 tblsp. sugar
½ c. butter or regular margarine
½ c. sugar
½ tsp. salt
3 eggs
1¼ c. sifted flour
2 tsp. grated orange rind
¾ c. fresh orange juice
½ c. water
⅔ c. sugar
¾ c. warmed orange marmalade

Dissolve yeast in ⅓ c. lukewarm water in small bowl. Stir in ½ c. flour and 1 tblsp. sugar. Cover; let stand in warm place until bubbly, about an hour.

Cream butter, ½ c. sugar and salt until fluffy. Add eggs, one at a time, beating after each addition. Add yeast mixture, 1¼ c. of the flour and orange rind. Beat with electric mixer at medium speed 2 minutes. Turn into well-greased 1½-qt. ring mold. Cover; let rise until doubled, 1 to 1¼ hours. Bake in 350° oven 35 minutes or until done. Meanwhile, combine orange juice, ½ c. water and ⅔ c. sugar in saucepan. Bring to a boil, stirring constantly. Remove from heat.

Remove bread from pan immediately; place on rack. Brush with orange syrup until it is all absorbed (about 15 minutes).

Brush with marmalade. Makes 10 to 12 servings.

CHRISTMAS COFFEE RING

1 c. buttermilk
¼ c. shortening
⅓ c. sugar
1½ tsp. salt
2 pkg. active dry yeast
¼ c. lukewarm water (110°)
4½ c. sifted flour
2 eggs

2 tblsp. melted butter or regular margarine
Honey Filling (recipe follows)
Vanilla Glaze (recipe follows)
red maraschino cherries

Heat buttermilk in saucepan until warm. Combine buttermilk, shortening, sugar and salt in bowl.

Sprinkle yeast on lukewarm water; stir to dissolve. Add yeast and 2 c. of the flour to buttermilk mixture. Beat with electric mixer at medium speed 2 minutes, or until smooth. Blend in eggs. Gradually add enough remaining flour to make a soft dough. Knead on floured surface until dough is smooth and satiny, about 5 minutes.

Place in greased bowl, turning dough over once to grease top. Cover and let rise until doubled, 1 to 1¼ hours.

Punch down dough. Divide in half. Roll out each half into a 10-inch square. Brush with butter. Top each with half of Honey Filling. Roll up like jelly roll; pinch edge. Cut in 1-inch slices. Layer slices, cut side down, in greased 10-inch tube pan with solid bottom. Cover; let rise until dough reaches the top of pan, about an hour.

Bake in 350° oven 45 minutes or until done, covering with aluminum foil the last 20 minutes to prevent overbrowning. Remove from pan; cool on rack. Drizzle with Vanilla Glaze; decorate with cherries. Makes 12 servings.

Honey Filling: Combine ⅓ c. raisins, ⅓ c. chopped walnuts, ¼ c. sugar, 1 tsp. ground cinnamon, 1 tblsp. grated orange rind, 1 tblsp. orange juice and ½ c. honey in bowl; mix well.

Vanilla Glaze: Combine 1 c. sifted confectioners sugar with 1 tblsp. milk and 1 tsp. vanilla in bowl; beat until smooth.

Classic Ways with Cheese

For a happy change from the usual round of holiday sweets, gather a group of friends around a simmering pot of cheese fondue.

These four versions—made with sharp Cheddar, Swiss, brick and Colby cheeses—are fashioned after the classic Swiss fondue. Since these don't contain wine, there's no need to prepare them at the last minute; each may be made in advance and gently reheated just before you're ready to dip in. Serve with lots of crusty bread and raw vegetables such as sliced celery, carrots and mushrooms.

Or, use these same cheeses as appetizers—sliced, or softened and combined with nutmeats and seasonings into plump cheese balls. Recipes for Cheddar Cheese Ball, Blue Cheese Ball and Salmon-Pecan Ball follow the fondue recipes.

BACON-CHEDDAR FONDUE

5 strips bacon
1 c. chopped onion
1 clove garlic, finely minced
**1 (10½-oz.) can condensed
 cream of mushroom soup**
1 c. milk
**1½ lb. sharp Cheddar cheese,
 shredded**
1 tsp. Worcestershire sauce
1 tsp. dry mustard
3 dashes hot pepper sauce
minced fresh parsley
**French or Italian bread, cut in
 1½-inch cubes**
assorted raw vegetables

Fry bacon until crisp and brown in heavy 3-qt. saucepan. Drain on paper towels. Crumble bacon; set aside.

Reserve ¼ c. of the bacon drippings. Add onion and garlic to drippings; saute until tender (do not brown).

Add soup. Slowly stir in milk. Cook over medium heat, blending until smooth.

Add cheese, a little at a time, stirring until melted. Add bacon, reserving some for garnish. Add Worcestershire sauce, mustard and hot pepper sauce.

Pour into fondue pot and keep warm. Garnish with bacon and parsley. Provide bread cubes and slices of raw vegetables to dip in fondue. If mixture becomes too thick, stir in a little hot milk. Makes 5 cups.

DOUBLE CHEESE FONDUE

2 tblsp. minced celery
**¼ c. melted butter or regular
 margarine**
¼ c. flour
1 c. milk
1 c. light cream
¾ lb. Swiss cheese, shredded
¼ lb. brick cheese, shredded
1 tsp. Worcestershire sauce
¼ tsp. dry mustard
¼ tsp. onion salt
1/16 tsp. cayenne pepper
**French or Italian bread, cut in
 1½-inch cubes**
assorted raw vegetables

Saute celery in melted butter in heavy 3-qt. saucepan until tender (do not brown). Stir in flour. Gradually stir in milk and cream. Cook, stirring, until thick.

Slowly add cheeses; stir until melted. Add the remaining ingredients.

Pour into fondue pot and keep warm. Provide bread cubes and slices of raw vegetables to dip in fondue. If mixture becomes too thick, stir in a little hot milk. Makes 4 cups.

GOLDEN PIZZA FONDUE

1 tblsp. minced onion
1 clove garlic, finely minced
**2 tblsp. melted butter or regular
 margarine**
3 tblsp. flour
1 (1-lb.) can stewed tomatoes
½ tsp. dried basil leaves
½ tsp. dried oregano leaves
⅛ tsp. cayenne pepper
⅛ tsp. pepper
½ c. milk
**1 lb. mild Cheddar cheese,
 shredded**
**1 tblsp. Parmesan cheese,
 grated**
**French or Italian bread, cut in
 1½-inch cubes**
assorted raw vegetables

(continued on p. 23)

Saute onion and garlic in melted butter in heavy 3-qt. saucepan until tender (do not brown). Add flour. Stir in tomatoes, breaking them up with spoon. Add basil, oregano, cayenne pepper and pepper. Cook over medium heat, stirring for 5 minutes. Slowly stir in milk.

Add Cheddar cheese, a little at a time, stirring, until melted. Add Parmesan cheese.

Pour into fondue pot and keep warm. Provide bread cubes and slices of raw vegetables to dip in fondue. If mixture becomes too thick, stir in a little hot milk. Makes about 4 cups.

CLAM CHEESE FONDUE

2 (6½-oz.) cans minced clams
milk
2 tblsp. minced onion
2 tblsp. minced celery
3 tblsp. melted butter or regular
**   margarine**
¼ c. flour
½ lb. Colby cheese, shredded
½ lb. brick cheese, shredded
2 tsp. Worcestershire sauce
French or Italian bread, cut in
**   1½-inch cubes**
assorted raw vegetables

Drain clams, reserving broth. Add enough milk to reserved broth to make 2 cups.

Saute onion and celery in melted butter in a heavy 3-qt. saucepan until tender (do not brown). Stir in flour. Gradually stir in reserved broth mixture. Cook over medium heat, stirring constantly, until thickened.

Add cheeses, a little at a time, stirring until melted. Add clams and Worcestershire sauce.

Pour into fondue pot and keep warm. Provide bread cubes and slices of raw vegetables to dip in fondue. If mixture becomes too thick, stir in a little hot milk. Makes about 4 cups.

CHEDDAR CHEESE BALL

1 lb. sharp Cheddar cheese,
**   shredded**
2 oz. blue cheese, crumbled
2 tblsp. Worcestershire sauce
1 tblsp. finely chopped onion
½ c. mayonnaise
5 drops hot pepper sauce
1 c. finely chopped walnuts
¼ c. chopped fresh parsley
½ tsp. paprika
assorted crackers

Combine cheeses, Worcestershire sauce, onion, mayonnaise and hot pepper sauce. Mix well. Chill for 2 hours.

Shape chilled mixture into a ball. Combine walnuts, parsley and paprika. Roll cheese ball in walnut mixture. Wrap in aluminum foil and chill until serving time. Serve with crackers. Makes 1 cheese ball.

BLUE CHEESE BALL

½ c. chopped walnuts
1 (8-oz.) pkg. cream cheese,
**   softened**
4 oz. blue cheese, crumbled
1 tblsp. chopped pimientos
1 tblsp. minced green pepper
¼ tsp. garlic powder
assorted crackers

Spread walnuts in shallow baking pan.

Toast in 350° oven 9 minutes, stirring occasionally, until golden brown. Cool slightly.

Beat cream cheese in bowl until smooth and creamy, using electric mixer at medium speed. Blend in blue cheese. Stir in pimientos, green pepper and garlic powder. Chill until firm.

Shape chilled mixture into a ball. Roll in toasted walnuts. Wrap in aluminum foil and chill at least an hour. Serve with crackers. Makes 1 cheese ball.

SALMON-PECAN BALL

1 (1-lb.) can salmon, drained
**   and flaked**
1 (8-oz.) pkg. cream cheese,
**   softened**
1 tblsp. lemon juice
1 tblsp. grated onion
1 tsp. horseradish
¼ tsp. salt
½ c. chopped pecans
⅓ c. chopped fresh parsley
assorted crackers

Combine salmon with cream cheese, lemon juice, onion, horseradish and salt; mix well. Chill for 2 hours.

Shape chilled mixture into a ball. Roll in combined pecans and parsley. Wrap in aluminum foil and chill until serving time. Serve with assorted crackers. Makes 1 cheese ball.

Invite a group of friends to dip chunks of French bread into this creamy Bacon-Cheddar Fondue.

Creative Cookies

Cookie-making is an event that even the youngest child can enjoy, and it's an occasion that's even more special when each cookie becomes a hand-painted original.

Artistic talent isn't required—all that's needed are liquid food colors, a basic butter cookie recipe, a few small brushes and some cookie cutters. The simplest shapes are often the most eye-catching, and ideas for decorations can be copied from gift wrappings or developed on the spot. The ones that are just too pretty to eat can be tucked into a gift box or hung on the tree. Recipes follow for the Hand-Painted Butter Cookies, pictured at right, plus four more cookies to serve at home or present as gifts—each one a creation from your kitchen.

HAND-PAINTED BUTTER COOKIES

1½ c. butter
1 c. sugar
2 eggs
1 tsp. grated lemon rind
4½ c. sifted flour
¼ tsp. salt
food colors

Cream together butter and sugar in bowl until light and fluffy, using electric mixer at medium speed. Add eggs and lemon rind; beat well.

Sift together flour and salt; add gradually to the creamed mixture. Cover and refrigerate dough 3 to 4 hours.

Roll out a portion of dough on lightly floured surface to ⅛-inch thickness and cut in desired shapes. Place on greased baking sheet.

Bake in 400° oven 6 to 8 minutes or until golden brown. Remove cookies from oven.

If you wish to use cookies as tree ornaments, make a small hole by twisting a toothpick through each cookie near the top. Cool slightly. Remove cookies from baking sheet and cool on racks. Makes about 6 dozen.

To decorate: Pour food colors into small saucers, adding a few drops of water. You can make many beautiful colors by mixing the basic colors. Use narrow brushes for fine lines, wider brushes for large areas. (Rinse brush in water when you change colors so that colors will be clear and not murky.) With colors of your choice, paint designs on the cookies. To hang, thread narrow, colored cord through the hole in each cookie.

CHRISTMAS JEWELS

1 c. butter
½ c. sugar
3 hard-cooked egg yolks
1 tsp. vanilla
2 c. sifted flour
strawberry or currant jelly

Cream together butter and sugar in bowl until light and fluffy. Break up egg yolks and beat into creamed mixture; blend well. Add vanilla.

Gradually stir in flour. Chill 1 hour. Shape dough into 1-inch balls and place 1 inch apart on ungreased baking sheet. Make a small hollow in top of each cookie with finger.

Bake in 375° oven 10 minutes. Remove from oven and fill hollows with jelly. Return to oven and bake 1 or 2 more minutes to set jelly. Makes 5 dozen.

ALMOND-RASPBERRY BARS

1½ c. sifted flour
½ c. sugar
½ tsp. baking powder
½ tsp. ground cinnamon
½ c. butter or regular margarine
½ c. ground blanched almonds
1 egg
½ tsp. almond extract
¾ c. raspberry jam
Vanilla Icing (recipe follows)

Sift together flour, sugar, baking powder and cinnamon into bowl. Cut in butter with pastry blender until mixture is crumbly. Add almonds, egg and almond extract; mix well. Spread half of dough in an 8-inch square on waxed paper. Chill in refrigerator. Meanwhile, press remaining dough in greased 8-inch square

baking pan. Spread with jam. Top with chilled dough.

Bake in 350° oven 35 to 40 minutes or until golden brown. Cool in pan on rack. When cool, drizzle with Vanilla Icing. Cut into 2½x¾-inch bars. Makes about 2 dozen.

Vanilla Icing: Combine ½ c. sifted confectioners sugar, 2 tsp. milk and ¼ tsp. almond extract in bowl. Beat until smooth.

CANDIED FRUIT BARS

4 eggs, beaten
½ c. melted shortening
½ tsp. vanilla
1½ c. sifted flour
1¾ c. sugar
1 tsp. baking powder
½ tsp. salt
1½ c. mixed candied fruit
Orange Frosting (recipe
follows)

Combine eggs with shortening and vanilla in bowl. Beat with electric mixer at high speed until thick and lemon-colored.

Sift together flour, sugar, baking powder and salt. Reserve ¼ c. of the flour mixture; mix with candied fruit. Gradually stir remaining dry ingredients into eggs; mix well. Add floured candied fruit. Spread mixture in a greased 13x9x2-inch baking pan.

Bake in 350° oven 30 minutes. While warm, frost with Orange Frosting. Cool in pan on rack. Cut into 3x1-inch bars. Makes about 3 dozen.

Orange Frosting: Combine 1 c. sifted confectioners sugar, 1½ tblsp. orange juice and ½ tsp. grated orange rind in bowl. Beat until smooth.

JUMBO OATMEAL-PEANUT BUTTER COOKIES

¾ c. butter or regular margarine
½ c. peanut butter
1 c. sugar
1 c. brown sugar, firmly packed
2 eggs
¼ c. milk
1 tsp. vanilla
2 c. sifted flour
1 tsp. baking soda
1 tsp. salt
1 tsp. ground cinnamon
1½ c. quick-cooking oats
1 c. raisins

Cream together butter, peanut butter, sugar and brown sugar in bowl until light and fluffy, using electric mixer at medium speed. Add eggs, one at a time, beating well after each addition. Blend in milk and vanilla.

Sift together flour, baking soda, salt and cinnamon. Stir dry ingredients into creamed mixture; blend well. Stir in oats and raisins. Drop mixture by tablespoonfuls, about 2 inches apart, onto greased baking sheets.

Bake in 350° oven 15 minutes or until golden brown. Remove from baking sheets; cool on racks. Makes 3 dozen (3-inch) cookies.

One basic fondant recipe makes the Almond-Studded Log at bottom left as well as the assortment of candies pictured in the center: a rosy mound of Fondant Balls surrounded by rings of Stuffed Dates, Candied Fruit Squares and Peppermint Pinwheel Patties. Also shown, clockwise from left, are Buttery Almond Brittle, Crystal Mint Drops and Deluxe Peanut Butter Fudge.

The Sweetest of the Sweets

One of the most welcome gifts that you can give to someone with a sweet tooth is a box of homemade candies. Even without cooking, you can make eight beautiful candies from one basic fondant recipe. The fondant can be used to turn out mints in pretty pastels, stuffed dates, tiny balls coated with sparkling red sugar, candied fruit squares, stuffed pecan halves, peppermint pinwheels and two handsome logs, one flavored with caramel and pecans and the other studded with almonds.

For veteran candy-makers, recipes follow for Crystal Mint Drops, Buttery Almond Brittle, Deluxe Peanut Butter Fudge and New Orleans Pralines. These recipes must be cooked to exact temperatures, and for best results they should be made on a clear, bright day—often they do not turn out as well on cloudy days when the humidity is high.

EASY FONDANT CANDIES

3 (1-lb.) boxes confectioners sugar
1 c. melted butter or regular margarine
1 (14-oz.) can sweetened condensed milk (not evaporated)

Sift 2 lb. of the confectioners sugar into mixing bowl. Add butter and sweetened condensed milk, mixing well with wooden spoon. Sift and knead in remaining 1 lb. confectioners sugar. This makes 4 lb. fondant. Divide fondant into fourths. Flavor and shape fondant as desired. (See variations that follow.)
To store: Wrap in plastic wrap or aluminum foil and refrigerate for up to 6 weeks.

Candied Fruit Squares: Use 1 lb. fondant. Knead in 1 tsp. vanilla and ½ c. finely chopped mixed candied fruit. Roll out on waxed paper lightly dusted with sifted confectioners sugar to 10x5-inch rectangle. Cut into 1¼-inch squares, using wet knife. Cut 16 red candied cherries in half. Top each square with a cherry half. Makes 32 pieces.

Stuffed Dates: Use 1 lb. fondant. Knead in 1 tsp. vanilla. Shape into 160 small logs, about 1¼x¼ inches. Slit 160 dates (about 2 lb.) lengthwise, using scissors or sharp knife. Place fondant logs in dates. Roll each stuffed date in sugar. Makes 160.

Peppermint Pinwheel Patties: Use 1 lb. fondant. Knead in 1 tsp. peppermint extract. Divide fondant in half. Knead 4 drops green food coloring into half of the fondant.

Roll out green fondant on waxed paper lightly dusted with sifted confectioners sugar to 10x7½-inch rectangle. Repeat with white fondant, rolling out on another piece of waxed paper. Invert white fondant on green fondant and peel off waxed paper. Roll up like a jelly roll, starting at wide end and peeling off waxed paper as you roll. Wrap in plastic wrap and refrigerate until firm, about 2 hours. Cut in ¼-inch slices. Makes 40 patties.

Pastel Mint Patties: Use 1 lb. fondant. Knead in 1 tsp. peppermint extract and 4 drops red or yellow food coloring. Roll out on waxed paper dusted with sifted confectioners sugar to ⅛-inch thickness. Cut with 1½-inch cookie cutter. (You can substitute 2 tsp. wintergreen extract for peppermint extract and tint fondant with 4 drops green food coloring.) Makes 52 patties.

Fondant Balls: Use 1 lb. fondant. Knead in 1 tsp. vanilla. Shape fondant into ¾-inch balls. Roll in colored decorating sugar or in multi-colored sprinkles. Makes 56 balls.

Stuffed Pecan Halves: Use 1 lb. fondant. You will need about ¾ lb. small pecan halves. Knead 1 tsp. vanilla into fondant. Shape into 136 (½-inch) balls. Press each fondant ball between 2 small pecan halves. Makes 136 pieces.

Caramel Nut Logs: Use 1 lb. fondant. Knead in ½ tsp. vanilla. Divide in half; shape each half into a 5½-inch log. Combine 24 caramels with 2 tblsp. water in top of double boiler. Place over boiling water and heat until melted. Remove from heat. Place 1 fondant log on greased baking sheet. Spread with half of melted caramel. Immediately roll in 1 c. chopped pecans. Repeat with remaining log. Cover and refrigerate until firm enough to slice. Makes 2 logs.

Almond-Studded Logs: Use 1 lb. of fondant. Knead in ½ tsp. almond extract. Divide in half; shape each half into 5½-inch log. You will need 1 (4-oz.) pkg. unblanched almond slices (1 c.) for decoration. Press almonds into log at right angles until entire surface of log is covered. Repeat with remaining log. Cover and refrigerate until firm enough to slice. Makes 2 logs.

CRYSTAL MINT DROPS

2 c. sugar
1 c. light corn syrup
½ c. water
½ tsp. red food coloring
1 tsp. peppermint extract

Combine sugar, corn syrup and water in heavy 2-qt. saucepan. Cook over medium heat, stirring constantly, until mixture comes to a boil. Continue cooking, without stirring, until mixture reaches 300° (hard crack stage).

Remove from heat. Add red food coloring and peppermint extract. Mix well. Drop mixture from tip of teaspoon onto oiled baking sheets to form 1¼-inch disks.

If the syrup hardens before all the candy is dropped, return to low heat long enough to melt the candy mixture, stirring occasionally.

Makes 110 disks, about 1¾ pounds.

BUTTERY ALMOND BRITTLE

½ c. dark corn syrup
2 c. sugar
⅓ c. water
¼ tsp. salt
3 tblsp. butter or regular margarine
1 tsp. vanilla
1 c. blanched almond halves

Combine corn syrup, sugar, water, salt and butter in heavy 3-qt. saucepan. Cook over medium heat, stirring constantly, until mixture comes to a boil. Continue cooking, stirring frequently, until mixture reaches 300° (hard crack stage).

Remove from heat. Stir in vanilla and almond halves. Pour into buttered 15½x10½x1-inch jelly roll pan. Cool completely.

Invert pan and tap on bottom to release brittle. Break into irregular-shaped pieces. Makes 1½ pounds.

DELUXE PEANUT BUTTER FUDGE

2 c. sugar
⅔ c. milk
1 c. smooth peanut butter
1 (7-oz.) jar marshmallow creme
1 tsp. vanilla
1 (6-oz.) pkg. semisweet chocolate morsels

Combine sugar and milk in heavy 2-qt. saucepan. Cook over low heat, stirring occasionally, until mixture reaches 236° (soft ball stage).

Remove from heat. Add peanut butter, marshmallow creme and vanilla. Beat to blend mixture. Pour into lightly buttered 8-inch square baking pan. Cool completely.

Melt chocolate morsels over hot water in the top of a double boiler and stir to blend. Spread over cooled fudge. Cut into 1¼-inch squares. Makes 36 pieces or 1¾ pounds.

(continued on next page)

NEW ORLEANS PRALINES

1 (1-lb.) box brown sugar
¾ c. evaporated milk
⅛ tsp. salt
1 tblsp. butter or regular
    margarine
1½ c. pecan halves

Combine brown sugar, evaporated milk and salt in heavy 2-qt. saucepan. Cook over medium heat, stirring constantly, until mixture comes to a boil. Continue cooking, stirring occasionally, until mixture reaches 234° (soft ball stage).

Remove from heat. Stir in butter and pecans. Cool on rack 5 minutes. With a wooden spoon, rapidly stir mixture until it thickens and begins to coat pecans, 2 to 3 minutes.

Drop mixture by heaping tablespoonfuls onto waxed paper-lined baking sheets. If candy becomes too stiff to drop easily, stir in a little hot water. Makes 18 (3-inch) patties, about 1½ pounds.

Breads and Jellies

In farm communities the giving of homemade bread at Christmas is as traditional as trimming the tree. Around Thanksgiving, country kitchens begin to send out the aroma of fresh-baked bread, and freezers begin to fill up with light yeast buns and firm-textured loaves flavored with fruits and nuts.

On the pages that follow we share some heirloom recipes for tea breads, buns and doughnuts to add to your own holiday food gift list, plus two quick jelly recipes.

CHRISTMAS FRUIT-NUT LOAF

2 c. sifted flour
1 c. sugar
1½ tsp. baking powder
½ tsp. baking soda
1 tsp. salt
¼ c. shortening
1 c. orange juice
1 tblsp. grated orange rind
1 egg, beaten
1½ c. chopped cranberries
    (fresh or frozen)
½ c. chopped walnuts
½ c. cut-up candied orange
    slices

Sift together flour, sugar, baking powder, baking soda and salt into mixing bowl. Cut in shortening with pastry blender or two knives until mixture resembles coarse corn meal. Add orange juice, orange rind and egg; mix just enough to moisten. Stir in cranberries, walnuts and orange slices. Pour batter into greased 9x5x3-inch loaf pan.

Bake in 350° oven 1 hour or

until golden brown. Cool in pan on rack 5 minutes. Remove from pan; cool on rack. Wrap loaf in aluminum foil and let stand 24 hours for easier slicing. Loaf also may be frozen. Makes 1 loaf.

BANANA TEA BREAD

2 c. sifted flour
3½ tsp. baking powder
¾ tsp. salt
⅓ c. shortening
¾ c. sugar
2 eggs
2 tblsp. orange juice
1 tblsp. lemon juice
1 c. mashed bananas
½ c. chopped walnuts

Sift together flour, baking powder and salt.

Cream together shortening and sugar in mixing bowl until light and fluffy, using electric mixer at medium speed. Add eggs one at a time, beating well after each addition.

Blend in orange juice, lemon juice and bananas. Gradually stir dry ingredients into creamed mixture, stirring just until blended. Stir in walnuts. Pour into well-greased 8½x4½x2½-inch loaf pan.

Bake at 325° oven 1 hour or until bread tests done. Cool in pan on rack 10 minutes. Remove from pan; cool on rack. Loaf also may be frozen. Makes 1 loaf.

ORANGE BREAD

2½ c. sifted flour
1 tsp. baking powder
1 tsp. baking soda
½ tsp. salt
½ c. butter or regular margarine
1 c. sugar
1 egg
1 tsp. vanilla
1 tsp. orange extract
1 tblsp. grated orange rind
1 c. orange juice
1 c. chopped dates
1 c. chopped pecans

Sift together flour, baking powder, baking soda and salt.

Cream butter and sugar in mixing bowl until light and fluffy, using electric mixer at medium speed. Add egg, vanilla, orange extract and orange rind; beat well.

Add the dry ingredients to creamed mixture alternately with orange juice, mixing well after each addition. Stir in dates and pecans. Pour batter into greased and waxed paper-lined 9x5x3-inch loaf pan.

Bake in 325° oven 1 hour 10 minutes or until bread tests done. Cool in pan on rack 10 minutes. Remove from pan; cool on rack. Wrap loaf in aluminum foil and let stand 24 hours for easier slicing. Loaf also may be frozen. Makes 1 loaf.

PUMPKIN DATE BREAD

3⅓ c. sifted flour
2 tsp. baking soda
½ tsp. baking powder
1½ tsp. salt
1½ tsp. ground cinnamon
½ tsp. ground cloves
½ tsp. ground nutmeg
⅔ c. shortening
2⅔ c. sugar
4 eggs

1 (1-lb.) can mashed pumpkin (2 c.)
⅔ c. water
⅔ c. chopped walnuts
⅔ c. chopped dates

Sift together flour, baking soda, baking powder, salt, cinnamon, cloves and nutmeg.

Cream together shortening and sugar in mixing bowl until light and fluffy, using electric mixer at medium speed. Add eggs, one at a time, beating well after each addition. Add pumpkin and water; beat well.

Add dry ingredients, stirring just until moistened. Stir in walnuts and dates. Pour batter into 2 greased 9x5x3-inch loaf pans.

Bake in 350° oven 1 hour or until bread tests done. Cool in pans on racks 5 minutes. Remove from pans; cool on racks. Wrap loaves in aluminum foil and let stand 24 hours for easier slicing. Loaves also may be frozen. Makes 2 loaves.

ORANGE SWIRL BUNS

2 pkg. active dry yeast
2 c. lukewarm water (110°)
½ c. sugar
½ c. butter or regular margarine
⅔ c. nonfat dry milk
2 tsp. salt
2 eggs
7¼ c. sifted flour
½ c. soft butter or regular margarine
1½ c. sugar
1 tblsp. grated orange rind
Thin Orange Icing (recipe follows)

Sprinkle yeast on lukewarm water in mixing bowl; stir to dissolve. Add ½ c. sugar, ½ c. butter, dry milk, salt, eggs and 2 c.

(continued on next page)

of the flour. Beat with electric mixer at medium speed (or beat with a spoon) until smooth, about 2 minutes, scraping bowl occasionally.

Gradually stir in enough remaining flour to make a soft dough that leaves the sides of the bowl. Turn out on floured surface and knead until smooth and satiny, about 10 minutes.

Place dough in greased bowl; turn over to grease top. Cover and let rise in a warm place until doubled, about 1½ hours.

Combine ½ c. butter, 1½ c. sugar and orange rind in bowl; mix well. Set aside.

Divide dough in half. Roll each half into 14x7-inch rectangle. Sprinkle each with half of sugar mixture. Roll up like a jelly roll, starting at long side. Cut into 12 slices. Place cut side down in 2 greased 13x9x2-inch baking pans, 12 rolls in each pan. Let rise until doubled, about 45 minutes.

Bake in 350° oven 25 minutes or until golden brown. Remove from pans; cool on racks. While still warm, glaze with Thin Orange Icing. Makes 24 rolls.

Thin Orange Icing: In a small bowl, combine 2½ c. sifted confectioners sugar and 3 tblsp. orange juice; beat until smooth.

SUGARED YEAST DOUGHNUTS

1 c. milk, scalded
⅓ c. cooking oil
3 tblsp. sugar
1½ tsp. salt
2 pkg. active dry yeast
¼ c. lukewarm water (110°)
1 egg
4 c. sifted flour
cooking oil
½ c. sugar
½ tsp. ground cinnamon

Combine milk, ⅓ c. oil, 3 tblsp. sugar and salt in mixing bowl. Cool to lukewarm.

Sprinkle yeast on lukewarm water; stir to dissolve. Add yeast mixture, egg and 1 c. flour to milk mixture. Beat with electric mixer at medium speed until smooth, about 2 minutes, scraping bowl occasionally. (Or beat with a spoon until batter is smooth.)

Gradually add the remaining flour, blending well. Roll out dough to ½-inch thickness on floured surface. Cut with floured doughnut cutter; place on floured waxed paper. Cover and let rise in a warm place until doubled, about an hour.

Pour oil into skillet or deep-fat fryer, filling one-third full. Heat to 350°.

Slide a few doughnuts at a time into hot oil, using floured pancake turner. Fry until golden brown, turning once. Drain well on paper towels.

Combine ½ c. sugar and cinnamon. Roll doughnuts in mixture. Doughnuts are best served warm. Makes 18.

EASY APPLE JELLY

4 c. bottled or canned apple juice
2 drops red food color
1 pkg. powdered fruit pectin
5 c. sugar

Combine apple juice, food color and powdered fruit pectin in Dutch oven; mix well. Bring to a boil over high heat, stirring constantly. Stir in sugar all at once. Bring to a full rolling boil and boil 1 minute, stirring constantly. Remove from heat. Skim.

Immediately pour into 6 hot, sterilized half-pint jars. Adjust lids according to manufacturer's directions. Cool on wire racks 12 to 24 hours. Check jars for airtight seals. Makes 6 half-pints.

CRANBERRY-BANANA CONSERVE

1 (1-lb.) pkg. fresh cranberries
1½ c. water
5 large ripe bananas
7 c. sugar
½ bottle liquid fruit pectin
1 tblsp. lemon juice

Combine cranberries and water in Dutch oven. Simmer for 5 minutes. Mash bananas to smooth pulp (should measure 3 c.). Add to cranberries along with the sugar. Bring quickly to a full rolling boil. Boil for 1 minute longer, stirring constantly. Remove from heat. Stir in liquid fruit pectin and lemon juice. Skim and stir conserve for 3 minutes.

Immediately pour into 5 hot, sterilized pint jars. Adjust lids according to manufacturer's directions. Cool on wire racks 12 to 24 hours. Check jars for airtight seals. Makes 5 pints.

Colorful packages and trims for food gifts can be made from potato chip canisters, a cone of Styrofoam, and containers for oatmeal, shortening and coffee; directions are included below. The silver gift box was made by decorating a ready-made foil box with gold braid and a self-adhesive bow.

Wrap-up:
The Finishing Touch

Women who live on ranches and farms seem to have a knack for personalizing their food gifts. One good cook packages her cinnamon buns on cooling racks tied with red ribbon. Another buys baskets at summer flea markets, then lines them with colorful napkins, fills them with loaves of tea breads and attaches fresh holly to the handles.

Many women use recycled materials to decorate their food gifts. A month or so before Christmas, they start to save boxes, canisters and jars, then wrap them in bright Christmas paper, colored tissue, fabric scraps and wallpaper remnants. Even the children help decorate, with braid and rickrack and paper stars.

A little imagination can transform a potato chip canister into a candy box—and an oatmeal box can become a bright pink elephant to delight a child. Directions for these and other packaging ideas follow.

PINK ELEPHANT GIFT BOX

MATERIALS

1 (1-lb. 2-oz.) oatmeal box
construction paper: bright pink,
   white, orange and yellow
6-inch yellow cord
4 corks, painted white
plastic bag with twist-tie

DIRECTIONS

You will need pink paper 13 inches long to wrap oatmeal cartons. If your construction pa-

(continued on next page)

per is not this large, glue pieces together as needed. Note that the lid will be covered separately so that it can be removed.

1. Cut pink paper 6½x13 inches and glue to oatmeal box, overlapping seams.
2. On pink paper, trace 2 circles, using lid as pattern. Cut out. Glue a circle to bottom of box; glue other circle to lid. Cut pink strip (¾x13 inches) and glue around rim of lid.
3. Trace patterns for elephant ears, mouth and eyes on white paper; cut out. Cut elephant inner ears from yellow paper; glue inner ears to ears. Glue eyes, mouth and ears to bottom of oatmeal box to make face.
4. Trace trunk pattern on pink paper; cut out; fold and staple end as shown in Step 1. Glue trunk to face as shown in Step 2.
5. Cut an X in center of lid; push cord through and knot to make a tail.
6. Glue corks to body of elephant to form legs.
7. Place plastic bag in box; fill with candies or cookies. Close with twist-tie. Place lid on box.

WHITE CHRISTMAS TREE

MATERIALS

5 (14x17-inch) sheets thin white paper, such as layout paper from art supply store
rubber cement
1 pack blue sequin flowers
yellow construction paper
1 (12-inch) Styrofoam cone

DIRECTIONS

1. Cut 19 pieces of white paper, 3½x13 inches each. Slash paper along one edge into strips ½ inch wide (see diagram). Curl strips with edge of scissors, curling 12 of the strips into tight curls and the remaining 7 strips

into loose curls.
2. Coat uncut edge of paper with rubber cement. Starting at top of tree, wind curled paper around cone in spiral rows. Use tightly curled paper first to cover upper part of tree; place curled edge up. Space rows as closely as curls permit to make tree full. Use loose curls on lower part.
3. Cut star from yellow paper. Glue to top of tree.
4. Glue blue sequin flowers to tree; place 1 in center of star.
5. Use tree to decorate a large gift box filled with homemade goodies. The recipient can use the tree as a centerpiece.

SANTA

MATERIALS

1 (1-lb.) coffee can; plastic lid
2 (14x17-inch) sheets thin white paper, such as layout paper from art supply store
construction paper: pink and blue
3 inches of thick red yarn
1 (10-oz.) red paper cup

DIRECTIONS

You will need paper 13 inches long to wrap coffee cans. If your paper is not this large, glue pieces together as needed. Finished gift package will open from the bottom, so keep lid on the bottom as you decorate.
1. Cut white paper 3¼x13 inches and wrap around bottom of can, overlapping edges; glue.
2. Cut pink paper 2¼x13 inches and wrap around top of can, overlapping edges; glue.
3. For beard and hat trim, cut 8 pieces of white paper, 3½x13 inches each. Slash paper along one edge into strips ½ inch wide (see diagram) and curl strips with edges of scissors.
4. Starting at bottom, glue 5

rows of the curled paper around can, overlapping rows to make beard (see Step 1).
5. Trace mustache on white paper; cut out and paste above beard.
6. Glue red yarn in spiral to make round nose, and glue above mustache.
7. Cut round blue eyes, ⅜-inch diameter; glue in place.
8. Cover top of can with white paper (use plastic lid for pattern) and wrap rim with curled paper so that uncut edge extends above can about an inch (see Step 2).
9. Coil remaining 2 curled paper strips, 1 inside the other, to make a pompon. Glue to inside of rim at bottom of paper cup. Glue cup to paper on top of can.
10. Fill can from bottom with cookies or candies. Cover with plastic lid.

GIFT CANISTERS

MATERIALS

round containers
gift wrap or self-adhesive plastic, such as Con-Tact
ribbons and bows

DIRECTIONS

1. Choose any round container that will hold the food you wish to package. For example, you might use containers used to package coffee, shortening, potato chips or frozen juice concentrate.
2. Cover printing on containers with plain or patterned gift wrap or self-adhesive plastic. To determine length of paper needed, wrap string around circumference of canister; measure string; add ½ inch for overlap.
3. Decorate plain papers with gold foil seals or honeycomb plastic ribbon (sold in hobby stores for weaving place mats). Decorate with press-on bows.

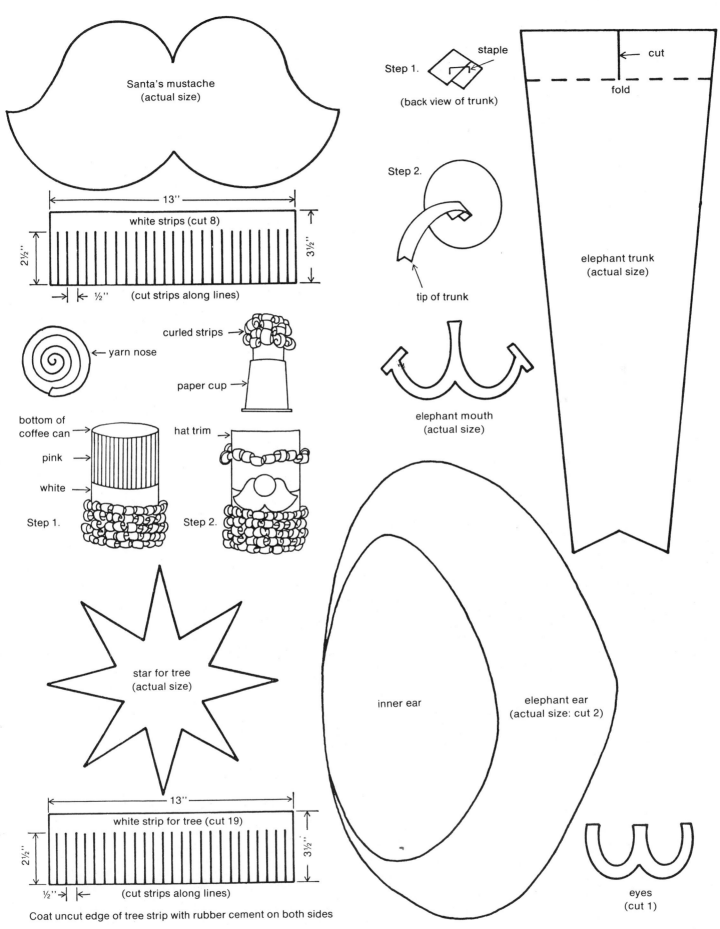

Santa's mustache
(actual size)

white strips (cut 8)

13"

2½"

3½"

½" (cut strips along lines)

Step 1.

staple

(back view of trunk)

cut

fold

Step 2.

tip of trunk

elephant trunk
(actual size)

← yarn nose

curled strips

paper cup →

bottom of
coffee can →

pink →

white →

Step 1.

hat trim →

Step 2.

elephant mouth
(actual size)

star for tree
(actual size)

inner ear

elephant ear
(actual size: cut 2)

13"

white strip for tree (cut 19)

2½"

3½"

½" → (cut strips along lines)

Coat uncut edge of tree strip with rubber cement on both sides

eyes
(cut 1)

33

CHAPTER 3

O CHRISTMAS TREE !

Trimming the Christmas tree may be the most popular holiday tradition shared by families around the country.

Some people insist on a freshly cut evergreen that casts a delicious fragrance around the room. Others simply unbox their "permanent" tree that's been stored in the attic. In either case, most of the ornaments hung on these trees have been collected over a lifetime of Christmases. They are like holiday memories, and each year a few new decorations—and memories—are added.

In many farm families there's another tradition, that of giving each child a special tree ornament each year. Then, as the children leave to begin their own homes, they take with them a boxful of happy memories.

You can buy gift ornaments, of course, but you'll find that those you make add an extra meaning to Christmas. As a Missouri woman explains:

"One of our happiest times at Christmas is decorating the tree with the many ornaments our family has made over the years. As we unwrap the items,

we find ourselves retelling the memories associated with each ornament."

The range of homemade ornaments is limited only by your imagination, supplies and skill. If you do needlepoint, for example, work a small design, stitch it to a backing and stuff it. If you crochet, work a lacy snowflake, then dip it in starch to stiffen it. With a jigsaw, you can cut simple shapes from wood, then paint them in bright colors or leave them natural.

"Maybe everything won't be perfect," says one mother, "but who cares? If it's a gift of love, you're not so concerned about perfection."

To stimulate your imagination, in this chapter we offer ideas for handcrafted ornaments of wood and fabric. Most of these are simple to make, and the children can assist with some.

And to help you better appreciate the freshly cut evergreen trees that will display so many of these ornaments, we begin with a brief chronicle of the long journey a live Christmas tree must make before it reaches your home.

From Seedling to Living Room

By NANCY WALKER

The bringing in of the Christmas tree isn't just the start of a celebration—it's the triumphant finish to a battle.

"Hold that door open all the way!"

Impatience made Dad's voice sound gruff. He started across our front porch toward me, his arms full of magnificent, scratchy evergreen. As the tree's huge bulk was squeezed carefully inward, branches grating on the door frame, its pungent pine fragrance preceded it, filling our living room in an instant and heading, unseen, for other parts of the house. In just a few minutes it was anchored in its stand. There it was—our Christmas tree.

In our home, as in more than 30 million homes across the nation, the carrying of a Christmas tree across the threshold is a holiday ritual. For many families, it's the unofficial beginning of Christmas.

But to a Christmas tree farmer, the bringing in of the tree isn't just the start of a celebration—it's the triumphant finish to a long battle.

For anywhere from seven to 15 years, a Christmas tree farmer battles against frost and drought and flooding and 20-foot snows; against the destructive nibbling of sharp-toothed mice and rabbits; against the diseases and fungi that can spread like wildfire through acres of young trees; and against increasing chemical, labor and machinery costs. The battle is won each time a nicely shaped, fresh-smelling evergreen is carried over a threshold.

A Christmas tree's long journey to your living

35

room begins when it's a seedling. Few of the more than 10,000 Christmas tree farmers in the United States grow their own seedlings; most buy them from commercial nurseries. Because the trees grow so slowly, most farmers get a head start by buying two- or three-year-old seedlings which, depending on the variety, are only eight to 15 inches tall. Experienced tree farmers purchase and plant three seedlings for each tree they plan to harvest.

First the spindly little seedlings are placed six inches apart in a transplant bed, and here they remain for two or three years until they reach a height of between two and three feet. It is during this stage that bad weather can be especially dangerous. Below-freezing temperatures in late spring, when the little trees are struggling to grow, can kill all the new buds on a tree's branches and prevent any growth that year. An even more serious threat is drought.

For those seedlings that survive the two years in the seedling bed, the next move can be traumatic. After their root systems have become fairly well developed, trees that will be cut once they mature are transplanted into fields that have been cleared of all weeds and underbrush. Those trees that will be sold as potted, or balled-and-burlapped, trees—about 450,000 or 1.5% of the 32 million trees sold annually—are transplanted into pots, where they continue to grow until they are large enough to be sold. During this transplanting process, many trees die from shock.

To produce the highest number of top-quality trees, most Christmas tree farmers plant young trees at five-foot intervals in rows six feet apart. Without adequate spacing, crowded trees will shade each other, causing poor, off-colored growth and, eventually, "holes" in the faces of the trees. Growth rate from this stage on usually averages one foot a year, so trees must be frequently pruned to keep them well-formed and dense, with a proportionate amount of width for their height.

Once the young trees are in the field, mowing becomes a year-round project for the Christmas tree farmer. Fast-growing weeds can deform or even kill young trees by robbing them of sun, water and space. Unfortunately, it's not uncommon for small trees hidden by tall grasses to be accidentally mowed down in the process.

Diseases and insect pests also can prevent a tree from reaching your home. Most tree farmers attack disease and insects by spraying with pesticides at least once a year.

Robert Norris, who has been growing Christmas trees on his 122-acre farm in Onondaga County, N.Y., since 1962, remembers a year when his trees were hit by an infestation of pine needle scale, small prolific insect pests which attach themselves to the trees and suck out the juices. Norris decided to attack the problem with a highly specialized tool: a biological weapon.

"I had four gallons of ladybugs flown in from California," he recalls. "The directions said to keep them stored in a cool place until you were ready to put them out in the tree lots. So, when they arrived, I put them in my wife's refrigerator overnight. But one of those containers must have had a hole in it. The next morning, the whole inside of the refrigerator was covered with ladybugs!"

Eventually, Norris and his wife managed to scoop up all the escapees. But once out in the tree lots, the ladybugs again began to wander. Instead of staying in the Christmas trees, most went next door to a neighbor's corn field to feast on corn lice. The scale finally was conquered with conventional chemicals.

For years, the most popular height for a Christmas tree has been six to nine feet. A tree this size will fit "just right" into the average family living room. It takes a Colorado Spruce between 12 and 15 years to grow to a nicely shaped, mature tree of that size. A Scotch Pine takes eight to 10 years to reach maturity, and the faster-growing Douglas Fir "only" seven to nine years. In the last four or five years, demand for smaller trees has risen, which may be related to inflation or the increase in townhouses, apartments and motor homes. More and more trees sold are table-top size—3½ to 4½ feet—or "apartment size"—4 to 5½ feet. To meet this demand, trees often are cut prematurely.

Harvesting begins with a careful scrutiny and selection of trees. The cut trees are fed through a baler, which wraps them snugly in lightweight netting to protect their limbs against breakage and to make the trees easier to handle. After baling, the trees are piled in large stacks, then hauled away by the truckload to wholesalers or retailers.

Often, the farmers don't harvest all their trees. Many Christmas tree farms are "choose and cut" plantations where people come to cut their own. It costs less than buying a tree at a neighborhood corner lot or from the local scout troop, but a family may save very little after driving to the farm. Still, for many people, the nostalgia, the togetherness and the escape from the city into a wintry, pine-covered countryside is reason enough.

Some people like to choose their tree four or five months before Christmas. Robert Norris recalls one woman who visited his farm a few summers back. She spent a good deal of time wandering around the tree lots, pondering the qualities of each tree before at last making up her mind. It was only then that she realized she had brought nothing with which to tag her choice. Not wishing to lose her tree to another customer, she made a quick decision. Pulling off her garter, she hung it high on the tree to mark it as hers—and there the distinctive tag stayed for the rest of the summer until she returned to cut her tree.

This year, when you carry your own Christmas tree across the threshold, think for just a moment of the journey it's made, the history it has, and the countryside where it grew. Then, bringing in the tree might contain just a bit more of the magic of Christmas for you and your family.

Picking the Perfect Tree

What will you look for when you choose your Christmas tree? You may already prefer one variety of tree, either because it's traditional or just because it's common to your part of the country. And of course, you'll think carefully about the size, shape and color of your tree. But to select a tree that's just right for you and your family, you should also keep in mind some other characteristics that vary with each evergreen species.

Consider, for example, qualities such as needle length and shape, the way the branches grow, and the strength of a tree's limbs. The last is particularly important if you like to load down your tree with ornaments—you won't want it to droop under the burden. How well the tree retains its needles also is a consideration, and the sharpness of a tree's needles also should be noted, especially by parents of small children.

These four varieties of Christmas trees are among the most widely sold in the United States:

Douglas Fir: This native of the West Coast, also known as the Montana Fir, retains its needles well. Its needles are short, soft and pliable, and are dark yellow-green or blue-green. Its horizontal branches are more limber than those of other varieties and may sag under heavy ornaments.

Scotch Pine: When pruned and trimmed properly, the Scotch Pine can be made very bushy. It holds its needles, which are dark blue-green or grayish green, longer than most other species. The needles grow in clusters of two, are usually twisted, and are often longer than those of the balsam or Douglas Fir.

Balsam Fir: Also noted for good needle retention, this tree, which is common to the East coast, has short, flat, dark green needles usually rounded at the tips and soft to the touch. The tiny twigs grow at right angles to the branches, which are strong and well-suited to bearing decorations. The balsam has a delightful fragrance.

Colorado Blue Spruce (also pictured on p. 35): Always a favorite because of its lovely coloring, the Blue Spruce has one-inch pointed needles ranging in color from silvery green to blue-green. Its rigid, sharp needles extend at right angles from nearly all sides of its straight twigs.

37

Ornaments of Wood

Handcrafted decorations add special meaning to Christmas, whether they're hung from the tree or used to crown a holiday gift package. Make a set of ornaments for your own tree, and a few extras for gifts. Friends who receive them will remember you for many Christmases to come.

The delicate, swirling ornaments and the whimsical cutouts shown here all were made from scraps of pine; directions and patterns follow.

Wood Shavings

These ornaments made of natural pinewood shavings originated in Sweden. A fine soft grade of pine like that used by cabinetmakers works best, but any fine-grained pine will do.

MATERIALS

1-inch pine board with very little grain (for example, Idaho Sterling No. 5), cut in 8-inch lengths
wood plane (very sharp)
white glue
toothpicks
bobby pins or one-pronged hair clips
waxed paper

DIRECTIONS

1. Soak pine board in water for eight hours.
2. Place board in vise with 1-inch edge up.
3. Glide plane over 1-inch edge (along 8-inch length), in even, rhythmic strokes. Try to make 25 to 35 shavings before resting—a continuous rhythm is needed to make thin, even shavings.
4. Shavings will curl as they come off the plane, and can be used in that form. To turn curls in opposite direction or to make a different shape, soak shavings in water for 15 minutes.
5. Arrange curls in the shape of ornaments, following photos or using your own designs, by placing curls together flat on a piece of waxed paper. Hold curls in place with bobby pins or hair clips placed at strategic points. Allow to dry overnight and remove clips.
6. Place small amount of glue in saucer. With toothpick, apply glue where curls touch. Secure with hair clips. Keep flat on waxed paper at least 24 hours.
7. Tie thread at top of ornament to make loop for hanging. If you wish, glue tiny ornaments in center of each.

Wooden Cutouts

Several coats of wet-look spray paint give these colorful ornaments a high-gloss finish.

PAINTING TIPS

To spray-paint evenly, hammer a small brad into the top of ornament where screw eye will be. Tie a 10-inch string to the brad. When ready to paint, tie the ornaments on a clothesline some distance apart. Grip the brad of one ornament with a pair of small pliers so that you can maneuver the ornament as you spray the entire surface. Leave ornament on string to dry. After paint dries, replace brad with screw eye. To use spray paint for trim, spray a small amount of paint into a jar lid and dab on ornament with toothpick.

MATERIALS

pinewood scraps, ¼ inch thick
jigsaw
fine sandpaper
masking tape
enamel spray undercoat
enamel spray paints in colors
small can white enamel (for house roof and mushroom stem)
small can black enamel (for cat's whiskers and house chimney)
small paintbrush
toothpicks
small, stiff-bristle brush
colored construction paper
white glue
tiny screw eyes
gold thread

DIRECTIONS FOR HOUSE

1. Trace pattern, transfer to wood and cut out with jigsaw.
2. Sand edges smooth. Spray with enamel undercoat; let dry.
3. Sand lightly and cover the roof with masking tape. Spray rest of house in desired color of enamel. Allow to dry.
4. Remove masking tape. Paint roof white, using a brush.
5. After the white enamel dries, paint the chimney black.
6. Cut out door and window pieces from construction paper and glue into position.
7. To hang, twist screw eye into
(continued on next page)

top and add gold thread.

DIRECTIONS FOR CAT

1. Trace pattern, transfer to wood and cut out with jigsaw.
2. Sand edges smooth. Spray with enamel undercoat; let dry.
3. Sand lightly and spray-paint with desired color of enamel.
4. Cut cat's eyes, nose and mouth from construction paper. Glue into position.
5. Paint cat's whiskers, using a toothpick or small brush.
6. Paint flowers by dabbing paint in dots with toothpick.
7. To hang, twist screw eye into top and add gold thread.

DIRECTIONS FOR BIRD

1. Trace pattern, transfer to wood and cut out with jigsaw.
2. Sand edges smooth. Spray with enamel undercoat; let dry.
3. Sand lightly and spray-paint with desired color of enamel.
4. Cut wings from construction paper and glue into position.
5. Cut two eyes from construction paper (a paper punch can be used) and glue into position.
6. To hang, twist screw eye into top and add gold thread.

DIRECTIONS FOR MUSHROOMS

1. Trace pattern, transfer to wood and cut out with jigsaw.
2. Sand edges smooth. Spray with enamel undercoat; let dry.
3. Sand lightly and cover the stem with masking tape. Spray mushroom cap with red enamel.
4. After the red enamel dries, remove masking tape and paint the stem white, using a brush.
5. Dab on mushroom spots with a toothpick. The spots can be enlarged by smearing the paint in circles with the toothpick.
6. To hang, twist screw into top and add gold thread.

Patterns for Wooden Cutouts
(actual size)

Ornaments of Felt

The cheerful decorations pictured here are made from small pieces of felt—so if you look very closely at your scrap bag, you may find angels there.

These angels are designed to float in space, but Santa can either hang from the tree or stand—singly, or in company with a dozen look-alikes to form a jolly centerpiece. Directions and patterns begin on p. 45.

StocKings

The stockings we've hung out for display are just two examples of the personalized Christmas stockings you can make for family and friends. Add an initial of felt applique at the top left corner if you like.

To make full-sized stockings big enough to hold a generous cache of surprises, enlarge patterns as directed; finished stockings will be 20 inches long. For tree ornaments, make them in a smaller size.

42

Ice SKate

MATERIALS

tracing paper
felt: 18x30 inches white; 3x15 inches gray; 2½x14 inches black
3-ply crewel yarn: 12 yards orange; 6 yards dark gray; 7 yards light gray; 3 yards pink
2 yards pink velvet ribbon (¼ or ⅜ inch wide)
2 jingle bells
white glue

DIRECTIONS

(For directions on how to enlarge patterns and transfer pattern details to fabric, see p. 97. For directions on embroidery stitches, see p. 98.)

1. Enlarge pattern pieces and cut out.

2. From white felt, cut skate front, back and tongue. Cut skate blade from gray felt. Cut heel and sole from black felt.

3. Transfer embroidery details to front of the skate, using tracing paper.

4. With pink yarn, embroider heel lines and the line behind eyelets with backstitch.

5. To make bindings for skate and tongue, cut strips of white felt ¾ inches wide: 22 inches long for skate, 4 inches long for tongue. Press each binding in half lengthwise. Baste the long strip to top and front edge of skate, ending near bottom eyelet. Baste short strip to top curve of tongue. Sew bindings with backstitch embroidery, using pink yarn.

6. With dotted line as a guide, pin tongue under front skate edge and check its position by laying skate front piece over back piece—they should line up exactly. Secure tongue to skate with a few dots of white glue; then sew tongue to front of skate with invisible hand-stitches under edge of binding.

7. Cut out centers of eyelets (¾-inch holes); finish with button-hole stitch in light gray yarn.

8. Cut pink ribbon: 1 (3-inch) length, 2 (3½-inch) lengths; 8 (4¼-inch) lengths and 1 (24-inch) length. Starting with shortest piece on lowest eyelet, thread ribbons through eyelets; fold around front edge of skate; tack both ends on back. Pull long length of ribbon through top eyelet and tie in bow at front. Sew a bell to each end.

9. Glue sole to skate front and applique with black blanket stitches along top edge of sole (bottom edge will be blanket-stitched in step 10).

10. Glue gray blade to skate back. Lay skate front over back and pin. Sew them together by blanket-stitching all edges, using dark gray yarn on gray runner, black on bottom (sole) of skate, and light gray on white sole.

11. Braid 9 lengths of light gray yarn to make a loop for hanging skate; attach at top left corner.

12. With orange yarn, make a 3-inch pompon. Use the large-size pompon maker if you have one; or wind yarn around a strip of cardboard 1½ inches wide, slide a needle under yarn along one edge and draw it together. Cut yarn free on opposite edge; tie tightly. Attach to skate.

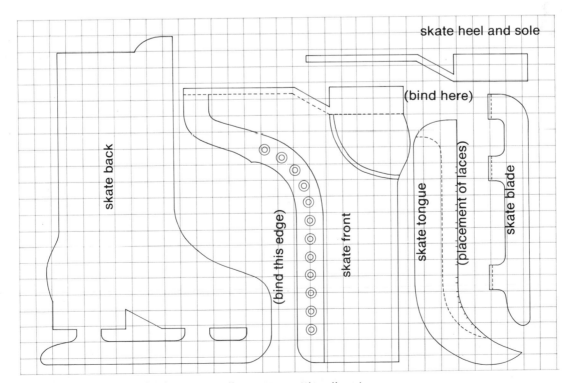

(1 square = 1 square inch; pattern lines are cutting lines)

Cowboy Boot

MATERIALS

felt: 18x30 inches dark grey;
　　12x18 inches tan
tracing paper
3-ply crewel yarn: 10 yards tan;
　　10 yards black; 2½ yards
　　white
white glue

DIRECTIONS

(For directions on how to enlarge patterns and transfer pattern details to fabric, see p. 97. For directions on embroidery stitches, see p. 98.)

1. Enlarge pattern pieces and cut out.
2. From gray felt, cut 2 complete boot pieces. Cut a tan vamp and a tan bootstrap.
3. Transfer embroidery design to front of the boot, using tracing paper.
4. Chain-stitch scroll pattern on boot front with tan yarn. Chain-stitch the vertical line with black yarn.
5. Dab a little white glue on back of vamp and press to boot front. (Dotted lines of pattern show placement, ½ inch from the bottom edge of the boot.)
6. Embroider top and bottom edges (but not sides) of vamp to boot with backstitch, using white yarn. Stitches should be about ⅛ inch long and ⅛ inch from edge.
7. Pin boot front to boot back and sew them together by blanket-stitching outside edges with black yarn. At top of boot, blanket-stitch front and back edges separately, to leave boot open.
8. Embroider boot strap around edges with backstitch, using white yarn. Stitches should be about ⅛ inch long and ⅛ inch from edge. Fold over top of boot and tack in place.
9. Braid 9 lengths of black yarn to make a small loop for hanging the boot. Attach at top left corner.

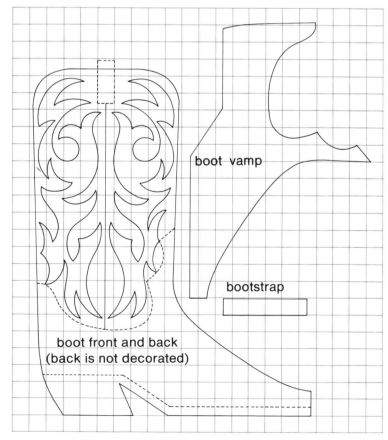

boot vamp

bootstrap

boot front and back
(back is not decorated)

(1 square = 1 square inch; pattern lines are cutting lines)

Angel

Felt is sold in small blocks as well as by the yard. Only a small amount of each color is needed for one ornament. Use the patterns on p. 46 to determine how much felt you need.

MATERIALS

pink felt and thread for body
red felt and thread for cheeks
paper punch (optional)
colored felt for gown; thread to
    match
embroidery floss for face (red
    for lips and nose plus another
    color for eyes)
crewel yarn and matching
    thread for hair
yarn or crochet-weight thread
    for tying pigtails
polyester fiberfill
6-inch length of lace to trim hem
2½ inches of pre-gathered lace
    to trim neck
white felt and thread for wings
nylon fishing line or light-
    colored thread

DIRECTIONS

(For directions on how to enlarge a pattern, see p. 97.)

1. Trace pattern pieces and cut out.
2. Pin body pattern to two thicknesses of pink felt; do not cut.
3. Machine-stitch around body close to outside edge of pattern. Work from A to B, leaving top of head open. Trim excess fabric to within ⅛ inch of seam. (The head will be stitched and trimmed later.)
4. From red felt, cut or punch two circles for cheeks. Hand-stitch cheeks to face; embroider features with floss.
5. Stuff body with fiberfill.
6. With pattern pinned in place, machine-stitch around head. Trim fabric to within ⅛ inch of seam.
7. Pin gown pattern to two thicknesses of colored felt. Machine-stitch down back (C to D) and along front (E to F), leaving top of sleeve to be stitched and trimmed later. Cut out rest of gown, trimming felt to within ⅛ inch of seams and using pattern as a guide to cut hem, sleeve edge and neck.
8. Hand-stitch 6-inch length of lace to bottom edge of gown.
9. Slip angel body into the gown through open neck and sleeve.
10. Machine-stitch top of sleeve and trim to within ⅛ inch of seam.
11. Hand-stitch 2½ inches of pre-gathered lace around neck.
12. To make hair, cut a 6-yard, 2-inch length of crewel yarn. Wrap it around a piece of cardboard 5½ inches long.
13. Slip yarn off cardboard and compress it to a 1-inch width at center. Machine-stitch along this "part" in the hair.
14. Hand-stitch yarn to angel's head along part. Arrange into pigtails; tie with yarn or crochet thread.
15. For wings, pin pattern to two thicknesses of white felt. Machine-stitch close to edge of pattern, and trim to within ⅛ inch of seam.
16. Hand-stitch wings to back of angel.
17. To hang, attach nylon line or thread to back of angel.

Santa

Santa's body is the same front and back; you determine the front when you add his face.

Use patterns to determine how much felt you need.

MATERIALS

felt in red, black, gold and pink;
    thread to match
embroidery floss in red (for
    nose) and black (for eyes)
thick white yarn; white thread
white fake fur for beard
white pompon for cap
polyester fiberfill
gold thread

DIRECTIONS

(For directions on how to enlarge a pattern, see p. 97.)

1. Trace patterns and cut out.
2. Pin body pattern to two thicknesses of red felt; do not cut.
3. Machine-stitch close to outside edge of pattern. Work around body from A to B, leaving cap and bottoms of legs open. Trim fabric to within ⅛ inch of seam. (Cap will be stitched and trimmed later.)
4. Cut face from pink felt. Cut or punch red circles for cheeks and hand-stitch to face. Embroider eyes and nose.
5. Stuff body with fiberfill.
6. With pattern pinned in place, machine-stitch around cap. Trim to within ⅛ inch of seam.
7. Cut buckle from gold felt and hand-stitch to front of Santa above yarn trim line.
8. For each boot, pin pattern to two thicknesses of black felt. Machine-stitch along outside edge of pattern, leaving top of boot open. Trim to within ⅛ inch of seam.
9. Fill boots with fiberfill, slip over Santa's legs and hand-stitch in place.
10. Hand-stitch white yarn trim to suit and cap. Sew pompon to tip of cap.
11. Cut beard from fake fur and hand-stitch in place.
12. To hang, add gold thread.

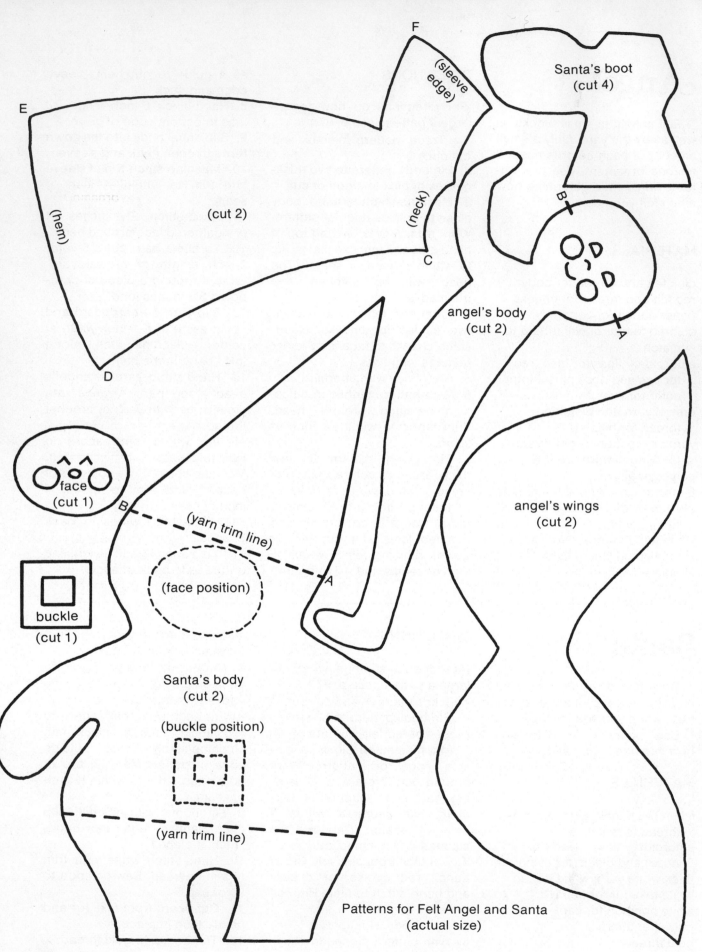

F

(sleeve edge)

Santa's boot
(cut 4)

E

(hem)

(cut 2)

(neck)

C

B

angel's body
(cut 2)

A

D

angel's wings
(cut 2)

face
(cut 1)

B

(yarn trim line)

(face position)

A

buckle
(cut 1)

Santa's body
(cut 2)

(buckle position)

(yarn trim line)

Patterns for Felt Angel and Santa
(actual size)

Ornaments of Calico

Even if you can't sew, you can create colorful ornaments like these with a few pieces of cotton and corrugated cardboard.

These ornaments are made like sandwiches: each one has two layers of fabric wrapped around cardboard cores and glued together. Only a half-dozen stitches are needed to secure the yarn that forms the flourishes. Since the finished ornaments are small—only about four inches long—they look best when they're made with small prints. A mix of prints and solids looks pretty, but no more than two prints should be used for any one ornament. Use the patterns to estimate the amount of each fabric needed.

MATERIALS

lightweight fabrics in small
  prints and solids
corrugated cardboard about ⅛
  inch thick (select tan, unprinted cardboard)
white glue
12 metal hair clips (to hold glued
  fabric in place)
single strands of colored wool
  crewel yarn
crewel needle

DIRECTIONS
FOR EACH ORNAMENT

(For directions on how to transfer pattern details to fabric, see
p. 97.)

1. Trace pattern and transfer to
two pieces of cardboard. Cut
out cardboard patterns. Next, divide both cardboard patterns into sections, cutting along solid
lines.

2. Choose fabric to cover each
section of pattern. Line up
matching layers so they will
sandwich together in mirror
fashion when finished. Cut fabric with ½-inch seam allowance all around cardboard; fabric will fold over edge of cardboard. Cover the front side of
cardboard shape with fabric.

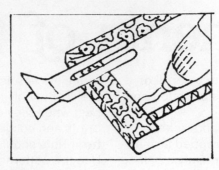

Fig. 1

Glue back of cardboard along
the edges, then fold fabric over
the glue (Fig. 1). Press and secure with hair clips until glue
sets. (Be careful not to get glue
on front side.) Snip off excess
folds at back if necessary for a
neat finish.

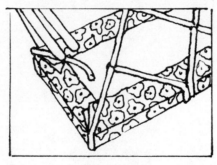

Fig. 2

3. Using dotted lines on pattern
as a guide, wrap yarn around
front of each section. Glue to
back, using hair clips to secure
(Fig. 2). Small circles on pattern
show where yarn should be
sewn through fabric and card-

board. Use a clip to hold yarn,
and glue so that yarn doesn't
work back through hole.

4. To sandwich layers together,
glue the back of each layer near
the edge. Press matching layers
firmly together. Press and pinch
cardboard where needed to
make a smooth fit. With needle,
push any loose-fitting fabric or
yarn between the sandwiched
layers.

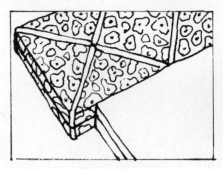

Fig. 3

5. To assemble the sections
and create a finished ornament,
apply glue to the edges of sections where they will butt together. Lay sections flat and press
firmly in place (Fig. 3). Wipe off
excess glue. Allow to dry.

6. To hang, take a 4-inch length
of the same yarn that trims ornament. Knot ends together to
make a loop. To attach, use a
needle to gently push knot between the two layers at the top
of the ornament. Secure knot
with a dab of glue.

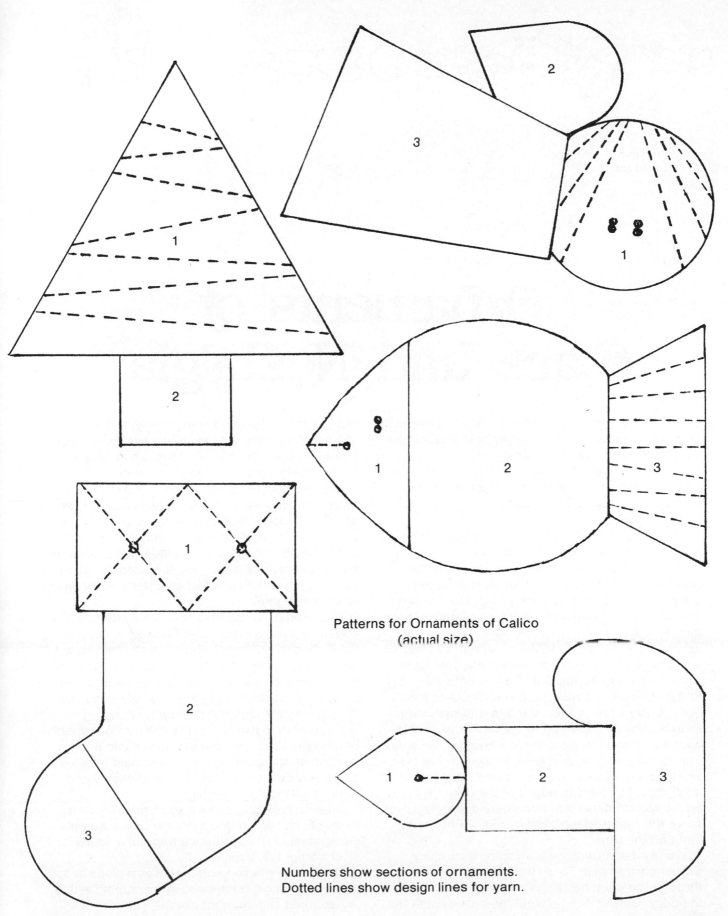

Patterns for Ornaments of Calico
(actual size)

Numbers show sections of ornaments.
Dotted lines show design lines for yarn.

Ornaments of Lace and Nostalgia

Satin, ribbons and lace lend a touch of romance and nostalgia to a Christmas tree, especially if the lace belonged to your grandmother.

If you aren't lucky enough to have antique lace, you may find remnants of delicate old lace at flea markets or garage sales. Of course, you can also use new lace.

Two of the ornaments shown here are made with crocheted doilies. To make a circular fabric ornament like the one pictured on the far left of the photograph, choose a small- or medium-sized doily. Using the doily as a pattern guide, cut two circles of satin large enough for a seam allowance plus a border (find a plate the right size and trace around it). Make a pillow-like ornament by stitching around fabric with right sides together, leaving a small opening for turning. Turn to right side, stuff and close opening with hand-stitches. Add the doily, using a few hidden stitches with matching thread; this will allow you to preserve the doily in case you decide to remove it for another use some day. (If doily is limp, press it with a warm iron between layers of waxed paper to add body before stitching.) The outside edges of the ornament may be tucked at intervals to add interest and help preserve the round shape. Add a loop of ribbon to hang on the tree.

We used a larger lace doily to cover a shiny Christmas tree ball. To do this, weave a thread through the openings around the outside edge of the doily. Gather doily around the ornament at the top and fasten thread. Arrange doily, taking tiny stitches if necessary, to keep fullness evenly distributed around the ball. To hang, add a loop of ribbon the same color as the ornament.

Lace edging looks great when it's gathered and applied to an ornament in a spiral design. We used an oval-shaped velveteen ornament, but a round ornament also is attractive and may even be easier to handle. First make a small pillow-like ornament, following previous directions, then add the gathered edging with hand-stitches. Finish with a satin loop for hanging.

A section of salvaged lace—from a tablecloth, a curtain or even a dress—can be used to copy the heart-shaped ornament. Ours is made with lace over antique satin, with the two fabrics handled as one. Make a pillow-like ornament following previous directions, then add gathered lace to outline the edge and a satin ribbon loop for hanging.

If you want to use one of the soft lace ornaments beyond the Christmas season, turn it into a fancy pincushion for a dresser top. It can hold needles and safety pins or be reserved for stickpins and other small pieces of jewelry.

Another idea is to make a soft ornament as a sachet to be tucked into a drawer or placed on a closet shelf. Just substitute a fragrant mixture for all or part of the stuffing.

Or you can treat one ornament as a piece of soft sculpture: hang it on the wall in a grouping with a few pictures and other interesting objects.

CHAPTER 4
DECK THE HALLS

As Christmas draws near, the air tingles with excitement and anticipation. Shoppers hum the familiar notes of Christmas carols as they hurry along the streets. Heavy-laden mail carriers trudge from house to house, delivering our season's greetings to relatives and friends. Families hold secret meetings to plan special foods and gifts. And everywhere, a myriad of colorful Christmas decorations blossoms forth. From floor to ceiling, inside and out, we decorate our homes, our churches, our offices, schools and stores in an outward expression of the joy we feel as we remember the miracle of Bethlehem.

Our heritage of Christmas decoration dates back to Roman times, when homes, public buildings and temples were decorated with holly, ivy and other greens on all festive occasions. The living greens, symbols of life, dispelled the gloominess of dark winter days and added to the gaiety of the celebrations. Through the centuries, bells, stars, candles, angels and other yuletide emblems have become part of our tradition.

In some homes, the glittering brilliance of colored baubles and tinsel expresses an urbane, sophisticated Christmas. But in this chapter, we share homespun decorating ideas that capture the individuality and craftsmanship of the maker while still bringing sparkle and cheer to each part of the house. These warm, carefully created adornments say "Merry Christmas" from the moment a guest sets foot on your doorstep.

We begin at the threshold, with simple and inexpensive ways to turn your doorway into a welcoming Christmas greeting. Then, walk with us through the rest of the house for a tour of decorating ideas to help you deck the halls of your own home.

Transform your vestibule or hallway with a glorious Christmas banner or wall hanging. Step into a dining room or kitchen made festive with arrangements of dried flowers, and set out a holiday feast on a table spread with a red and green patchwork tablecloth with napkin rings to match. Spread holiday cheer to other rooms all through the house with tabletop decorations and centerpieces made of natural materials such as cornhusks and wood.

'Tis the season to be jolly—and your home, bedecked in any of these joyful decorations, will reflect the true meaning of Christmas.

Threshold Greetings

Extend the glad tidings and good will of the holiday season to all who pass your door. Your threshold speaks a warm Christmas message to scurrying shoppers, hurrying neighbors and visiting friends and relatives when you decorate with one of these simple but imaginative ideas. For directions, turn to p. 102.

Banners and Baskets

The look of your hallway or vestibule gives arriving guests a feel for your Christmas spirit even before they've removed their hats and coats, and colorful banners like the ones pictured here will make a merry first impression. Add a sprinkling of baskets as shown here and on p. 57, overflowing with Christmas mail and brightly wrapped packages, to set the scene for a holiday visit.

Toy Soldier Banner

Unless otherwise noted, a machine zigzag stitch is used throughout for this banner. Patterns are included on p. 103.

MATERIALS

¼ yard red fabric
⅛ yard black fabric
pink, dark pink, blue and gold fabric scraps
white felt, 14½x34 inches
4 gold buttons
black fake fur, 8½ inches square
scrap of black leather-look vinyl
blue fabric, 22x46 inches
red and white striped fabric, 19x 40 inches (for backing)
2 gold curtain rods
thread to match fabrics
thick red yarn, 46 inches long

DIRECTIONS

(For directions on how to enlarge patterns, see p. 97.)
1. Copy patterns, enlarging as needed, and cut out.
2. Pin sleeve, jacket, and trouser pattern pieces to red fabric and cut out.
3. Pin strap, belt, cuff, jacket trim, boot and hair pattern pieces to black fabric; cut out.
4. Pin head and hand pattern pieces to light pink fabric and cut out.
5. Pin jacket and trouser legs to white felt; machine-stitch.
6. Pin straps, belt, jacket trim and boots in place; machine-stitch. Add gold buttons.
7. Pin sleeves, cuffs, hands and head in place; machine-stitch.
8. Cut out eyes (blue), nose (dark pink) and cheeks (red) from fabric scraps; machine-stitch to face. Add solid line of zigzag stitching in black for smile. Cut buckle from gold fabric; machine-stitch to belt.
9. Pin hair in place and machine-stitch.
10. Pin hat pattern piece to wrong side of fake fur; cut out. Pin in place and hand-stitch, turning edges under ⅛ inch.
11. Pin hat brim pattern to vinyl scrap; cut out. Pin in place on hat and machine-stitch with zigzag set at narrowest width.
12. Press sides of blue fabric panel under 1¼ inches and sew with a straight machine-stitch. Press top and bottom under 2 inches. Using a straight machine stitch, sew across panel 1⅛ inches from top and 1⅛ inches from bottom to form casings for rods.
13. Steam press and pin white felt panel in place on blue panel. Machine-stitch.
14. Hand-stitch red and white striped backing piece to back of banner. (This will not show from front.) Insert rods in casings; tie on red yarn for hanging.

Love Banner

Patterns for this banner are included on p. 104.

MATERIALS

felt: ⅜ yard yellow; 10½-inch square hot-pink; 10x18 inches royal blue; 5½x17 inches navy blue; scraps of light pink and brown; ⅜ yard white; thread to match
brown embroidery floss
2 bells
sandpaper
1 (½-inch diameter) dowel, 14 inches long
enamel undercoat spray paint
blue enamel spray paint
thick white yarn, 30 inches long

DIRECTIONS

(For directions on how to enlarge a pattern, see p. 97.)
1. Copy patterns, enlarging as needed, and cut out.
2. Pin banner pattern to yellow felt; cut out.
3. Pin heart pattern to hot-pink felt. Cut out and sew in place on yellow felt.
4. Pin pattern A and letter patterns to royal blue felt; cut out. Pin pattern B to navy blue felt; cut out.
5. Pin face, hand and feet patterns to light pink felt; cut out. Pin hair and sandal patterns to brown felt; cut out.
6. Sew letters and figures in place on yellow felt, using the photo as a guide.
7. Embroider eyes and soles of sandals with brown floss.
8. Cut a panel of white felt 12x 47 inches for banner backing. Sew yellow and white panels together, stitching down each side and using a ⅝-inch seam allowance. Trim to ⅛-inch seam allowance.
9. Sew around cut-out areas at top and bottom of yellow panel, using a ⅛-inch seam allowance. Cut away excess white felt to form three straps at top and bottom of banner.
10. To form a casing for the rod, sew ends of top three straps to back of banner.
11. Sew bells in place in curves at bottom of banner.
12. Lightly sand wooden dowel. Paint with enamel undercoat. Sand again lightly, and apply two coats of blue enamel.
13. When rod is dry, insert into casing. To hang, tie white yarn to ends.

(continued on next page)

Three Kings Banner

A simple running stitch is used for most of the appliqued pieces of this banner. Patterns are included on p. 105.

MATERIALS

⅜ yard white felt
purple felt, 9x12 inches
4½x6-inch blocks of lavender, turquoise and tan felt for robe trims and gifts
light pink felt, 4½x6 inches
gold felt, 4½x6 inches, for crowns and buttons
blue felt scrap for eyes of purple king
dark gold felt, 9x12 inches
brown felt scrap for eyes of gold king and hinge of gift C
blue-green felt, 9x12 inches
black felt scrap for eyes of blue-green king
thread to match felt colors
brown, black, gold and pink embroidery floss
⅜ yard hot-pink felt
3 (½-inch diameter) dowels, 13¾ inches long
1 (½-inch diameter) dowel, 14¾ inches long
sandpaper
enamel undercoat spray paint
white enamel spray paint
thick white yarn, 30 inches long

DIRECTIONS

(For directions on how to enlarge a pattern, see p. 97.)
1. Copy patterns, enlarging as needed, and cut out.
2. Cut three rectangles 8½x12 inches from white felt.
3. Pin robe and cap patterns to purple felt; cut out. Hand-stitch robe into position on piece of white felt.
4. Pin robe trim and cuff patterns to lavender felt; cut out. Hand-stitch into position.
5. Pin face and hand patterns to light pink felt; cut out. Pin gift A pattern to tan felt; cut out. Hand-stitch face, hands and gift into position, letting stitching of hands hold gift in position.
6. Pin crown A pattern to gold felt; cut out. Hand-stitch cap and crown into position, leaving top edge of crown unstitched.
7. Cut out 6 small circles of gold felt for buttons. With gold embroidery floss, make a French knot to attach each button to front of robe.
8. Cut two blue eyes; hand-stitch into position.
9. Using black and pink embroidery floss, embroider eyebrows, nose and mouth.
10. Repeat steps 1-9 for other two kings, substituting appropriate colors as shown in photo and as indicated in list of materials. Use B and C patterns for caps, crowns and gifts.
11. Cut a panel of hot-pink felt 12¼x42 inches. Hand-stitch completed kings to hot-pink felt background.
12. Cut a piece of white felt 12¼x42 inches for banner backing. Hand-stitch hot-pink panel to white felt backing: stitch down both sides the length of banner, ⅝ inch from edge of fabric; leave rod casings open. Trim to within ⅛ inch of seam.
13. Machine-stitch across bottom, top and between kings on stitching lines indicated. Seam lines should be ⅞ inch apart to fit a ½-inch dowel snugly.
14. To make casings, cut 2 pieces of hot-pink felt 2⅝x11½ inches. Pin one piece across bottom of banner, overlapping the backing; machine-stitch to back. Loop felt piece under bottom edge and up to front side; hand-stitch ⅝ inch from bottom edge of purple king. Repeat with second felt piece at top edge of banner.
15. Sand and paint all dowels with enamel undercoat. Sand again lightly and apply two coats of white enamel.
16. When rods are dry, insert into casings, placing longest dowel at top of banner. To hang, tie thick white yarn to the ends of the top rod.

Baskets of Glad Tidings

Use decorated baskets to hold incoming and outgoing mail and packages during the holiday season.

Choose baskets that are well-matched—the same color, the same weave or a similar shape. Fasten a card to each handle, so family members will know how each basket is to be used, and place in your hallway or vestibule.

MATERIALS

4 baskets: 2 small, 2 large
glue
velvet ribbon, ½ inch wide
velvet ribbon, 1½ inches wide
greenery and holly
beading wire
four white cards

DIRECTIONS

1. Glue velvet ribbon around edges and handles of all four baskets.
2. Attach sprigs of greenery and holly to baskets with wire.
3. Label two cards "In" and two cards "Out." Attach one "In" and one "Out" card to each of the two smaller baskets for mail. Attach remaining cards to the large baskets to hold packages.

A Big Splash for a Small Space

If your house or apartment is small—or if you want to create a big splash in a bedroom, den or family room—consider making a full-sized Christmas tree out of felt. The one shown here is eight feet tall, but it doesn't take up much space because it hangs flat against the wall.

The whimsical ornaments are done in bright colors, and each one is bordered in black to make it stand out. Ornaments for the panel are made with a design on one side only and are hand-stitched in place.

If you want to make these ornaments to hang on a real tree, you can use the same patterns—just make them double so that both sides have a design. (Directions follow.)

The double ornaments also can be used to hold small gifts when you turn them into stuffers, like the cat, rooster and ice cream cone designs shown below. These are simply double ornaments with an opening at the top to form a pocket. There's just enough room to tuck in a small surprise—a greeting, money or a gift certificate. After the gift inside is used up, the stuffer remains to decorate next year's Christmas tree.

Felt Tree

The finished panel is 8 feet high and 45 inches wide. A separate skirt extends 9 inches from the wall. All sewing is done by hand with small running stitches.

MATERIALS

3 yards white felt; white thread
3 yards green felt; thread to
    match
3 yards paper,
    for enlarging pattern
white marking pencil
curtain rod, 45 inches wide

DIRECTIONS

(For directions on how to enlarge a pattern, see p. 97.)
1. Fold white felt down center. From each edge, cut a strip 2 inches wide and 108 inches long (the full length of the felt). Sew one strip along each edge of the panel (on reverse side), using a single row of stitches along outer edge. This will prevent the felt from rippling.
2. Use paper to enlarge patterns for felt tree and skirt. Cut out patterns.
3. Fold green felt down center. Place tree pattern on felt, with center line of pattern on center fold. Outline pattern with white marking pencil. Carefully cut out double thickness of felt. Save remaining felt for floor section to be cut later.
4. Open felt tree. Center it on white panel 9 inches from top of panel. Be exact in placement. Baste through the two thicknesses along center folds; leave basting until tree is completed.
5. Pin outside edges of tree in

(continued on next page)

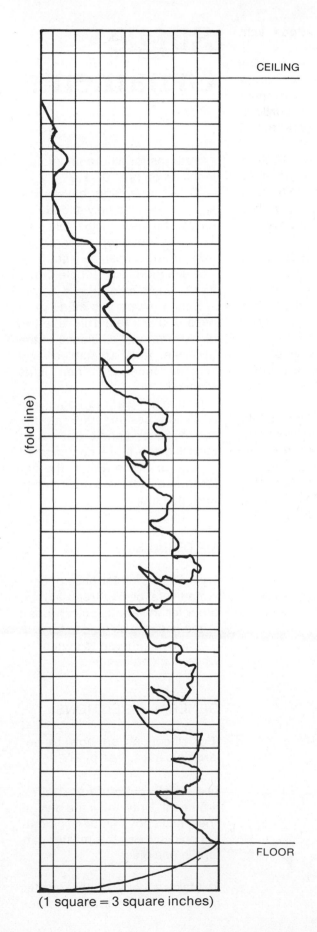

CEILING

(fold line)

FLOOR

(1 square = 3 square inches)

place. Sew along edges with small running stitches.

6. Pin completed decorations on tree. (Directions for ornaments follow.) Use running stitches around black borders, sewing through both green and white felt to secure.

7. At top of white panel, turn down 6 inches to wrong side. Sew along top edge with running stitches and again 2 inches from top to form a sleeve for curtain rod.

8. From bottom, measure up 6 inches (where tree is widest) and trim away white felt, following outline of tree. This makes an apron that lies on the floor when tree is hung.

9. Insert curtain rod at top of panel and hang tree, leaving 6 inches at bottom to curve onto the floor.

10. From remaining green felt, make skirt. Fold a length of felt, place paper pattern on top and cut. Place under tree apron with straight side along wall. (No sewing is needed.) This forms a base on which to set gifts.

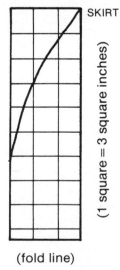

SKIRT

(1 square = 3 square inches)

(fold line)

Single Ornaments

Patterns for all ornaments are included on pp. 106-107.

These ornaments have a design on one side only and are intended for use on the felt tree. To make ornaments for a real tree—or to be used as a stuffer—see directions for Double Ornaments which follow.

Each ornament is made on a base of black felt. This is left in block form until all pieces of the ornament are assembled and stitched together. Then it is trimmed.

You might want to begin with a simple design such as the snowflake or candle before attempting the more complicated rooster or horse. Fill in the finished tree with rows of circles to form garlands.

MATERIALS

1 yard black felt for base of ornaments; black thread
other felt in various colors (use the patterns as guides for amounts); thread to match
white marking pencil

GENERAL DIRECTIONS

(For directions on how to enlarge a pattern, see p. 97.)

1. Enlarge pattern for desired ornament. Draw in all the design lines, and copy numbers indicating colors. Keep this master pattern in one piece.

2. Make a copy of the master pattern, adding all design lines and numbers. This copy will be cut apart.

3. Place master pattern on black felt and cut out a block, adding at least 1 inch margin on all sides. Set aside.

4. Choose colors for ornament. Trace design pieces on felt. Where two colors meet at the edges, one color should overlap the other. You must add extra felt to the bottom layer so it can be tucked under. (See pattern and directions for candle as a guide; dotted lines are used on this pattern as an example of how layers overlap.)

5. Follow directions below for each ornament you make. Then go on to Step 6.

Bird: Use master pattern to cut complete outline of bird on main color (1). Use small section pieces (2) to cut tail and wing from second color, and highlights (3) from third color. Cut eye (4) from another color.

Candle: Trace base (1) on one color. Trace candle section (2) on second color, adding extra felt at bottom (shown by dotted lines) to tuck under base. Trace flame sections (3) and (4), allowing extra felt to tuck under candle. (To slant candle flame to left, reverse all pieces of pattern before tracing.)

Candy cane: Use master pattern to trace complete cane on main color (1). Use small sections (2) to trace designs on second color, and (3) on third color. Follow master pattern to assemble. Areas marked (1) show where main color is exposed.

Cat: Trace outline of cat's body on main color (1). Trace head

60

and tail (2) on second color. Trace outline of eyes and nose (3), pupils (4) and whiskers (5) on other colors.

Circle: Cut from desired color.

Horse: Trace body on main color (1). Trace tail, mane and hooves (2) on second color. Trace saddle blanket (3) on third color. Trace saddle, harness, trim designs and eye on other colors. Before cutting, decide which pieces should overlap; allow extra felt on pieces that will be tucked under.

Note: Do not cut away area between horse's front legs. Instead, trace shape (9) on black felt; cut, and sew shape on top of horse design.

Ice Cream Cone: Use master pattern to trace outline of ice cream on main color (1). Trace sections (2), (3), (4) and (5) on other colors. Trace outline of cone (6) on one color, allowing extra fabric at top to tuck under ice cream. Trace highlights (7) on another color. After strawberry is in place, make French knots with gold thread to represent seeds. (For directions on how to make a French knot, see Appendix.)

Lollipop: Use master pattern to trace complete circle on main color (1). Use one swirl pattern piece, and trace it on contrasting colors (2), (3), (4), (5) and (6). These are all the same size. Trace stick (7), allowing extra at top to tuck under circle. Follow master pattern to assemble.

Pig: Use master pattern to trace outline of body on main color (1). Trace legs, ears and tail (2) on second color. Trace mouth, feet and trim (3) on a third color. Trace eye and tail curl (4) on

fourth color. Allow extra felt on tail and top ear to tuck under body.

Rooster: This design uses 11 colors, but it also can be made with fewer colors. Trace entire tail section on one color (1), adding extra felt where tail joins body. Trace tail feathers (2), (3), (4) and (5) on other colors. Trace all other design pieces. Before cutting, decide where pieces should overlap; allow extra felt on pieces that will be tucked under. You may want to cut each piece as you use it.

Sleigh: Trace outline of sleigh on main color (1). Trace trims (2) on a second color. Trace packages (3), (4) and (5) on other colors. Packages should overlap one another, and sleigh should overlap packages. Allow extra felt on package pieces for this.

Snowflake: Use master pattern to trace complete outline on main color (1). Use small shapes (2) to trace designs on second color. Follow master pattern to determine number of each shape you will need.

Treetop Ornament: Use master pattern to trace complete outline on main color (1). Trace sections (2) on second color; do not cut away centers. Trace sections (3) on third color.

6. Cut out design pieces. Assemble ornament on black felt. (Circles also are bordered with black.)
7. Begin with bottom layer and sew in place, using matching thread and small running stitches. Attach successive layers in the same manner.
8. After sewing is completed, trim black felt. Follow contour of the ornament, leaving a border at least ⅜ inch wide.

Double Ornaments

These ornaments have a design on both sides. Use patterns on pp. 106-107 to detemine how much fabric you need.

MATERIALS

black felt for base of ornaments;
  black thread
other felt in various colors;
  thread to match
white marking pencil
plastic ring, ½ inch in diameter
black buttonhole thread

DIRECTIONS

1. Follow Steps 1-7 above for making a single ornament; do not trim black felt.
2. Now, turn over all pattern pieces, and make the same ornament in reverse. This gives you a right side and left side for the ornament.
3. To add thickness, use the master pattern to trace a complete outline of the ornament on black felt. Treat this as a lining. Cut one for each side of the ornament, and sew in place.
4. Pin the two sides together, lining up designs exactly. Join the two sides along the black felt, close to the design. Use black thread and running stitches. For a tree ornament, completely close sides. For a stuffer, leave an opening at the top to form a pocket. After sewing, trim black felt, leaving a border at least ⅜ inch wide.
5. To hang, make a ring with black buttonhole thread as follows: Crochet around a ½-inch plastic ring, leaving 4 inches of thread at each end to sew ring to top of ornament. Center ring at top. (On stuffer, attach ring to one side of pocket only.)

Decorations for Dining

The rooms that are used by family and guests three times a day or more—the dining areas—are sometimes a bit neglected when it comes to ornamentation.

Here are ideas to dress up these rooms: a long-lasting bouquet for your dining room or kitchen table, a wreath of herbs for the kitchen door and a Christmas tree that can be placed in the corner of either room. All three of these decorations are made from dried weeds and flowers, which makes each one even more a conversation piece. Commercial versions carry substantial price tags, but make them yourself and they're almost free—yours for the collecting and drying.

To set off the holiday foods you'll be serving, cover the table in your dining room or kitchen with a festive tablecloth. Patterns and directions follow for a patchwork Pine Tree Tablecloth in Christmas colors, accented with a final festive touch—bright red Poinsettia Napkin Rings.

Dried Plant Arrangements

The plants used in all the arrangements shown were either air-dried or dried in sand. Directions for drying plants follow.

Begin collecting in summer and cut plants when they are at their best. Look for weeds such as goldenrod and pearly everlasting along roadsides and meadows. These plants make good filler materials, so collect them in great quantity, especially if you plan to make a weed tree. (Just be sure you don't plan to give such an arrangement to someone who suffers from hay fever!)

In each arrangement, try to coordinate colors: for example, deep red, purple and blue in one container and a combination of yellow, gold and orange in another.

Dried arrangements will last for several years. Their colors eventually do fade, but often you can refresh an arrangement by replacing a few blossoms.

HOW TO DRY PLANTS

To air-dry plants, simply tie them in bunches and hang them in a warm, dry, dark place such as an attic.

Plants that can be air-dried include: baby's breath, yarrow (or Achillea), pearly everlasting, goldenrod, dusty miller, statice, love-in-a-mist (the seed pod), fern fronds, hydrangea (fully mature), blue salvia, shepherd's purse, globe amaranth, dill seed pods, tansy blossoms, poppy pods, July lily pods, burdock, lavender, oats, rye, wheat and barley (plain or bearded), many grasses, herbs and teas (for fragrance), teasel (both dark brown and bleached) and joepye weed (bud stage).

To air-dry small strawflowers, pick them before they are fully open. Pinch each stem off behind the blossom, insert wire through center of flower, and hang to dry.

Some blossoms can be dried in sand. Beginners may have best results with small daisies, black-eyed Susans, single-blossom zinnias and marigolds.

Use dry, clean, fine-grained sand in an uncovered container. Leave only 3 to 4 inches of stem on each blossom. (You can rebuild a stem later, if necessary, by carefully inserting a wire and wrapping with florist's tape.)

Place blossom, such as daisy or zinnia, face down. Sift sand over and around blossoms until they are covered. Leave one to three weeks until dry. Remove gently from sand, pack in tissue paper or facial tissue and store in a dry place.

TO MAKE CENTERPIECE

Fit a piece of dry Oasis or other non-hardening floral foam into a container. Begin building arrangement with filler material, *(continued on p. 64)*

You can mix weeds with other plants and flowers to produce attractive arrangements like the centerpiece above and the weed tree at left. The weeds serve as filler material and actually make up most of the six-foot tree. In the wreath below, dried herbs are used with colorful flowers.

then add flowers and finally baby's breath.

TO MAKE HERB WREATH

Use a straw wreath as a base and attach dried herbs, plants and flowers with florist's pins. Decorate with a bird or a bow.

MATERIALS FOR TREE

wooden bucket (or other container, about 15 inches in diameter)
chicken wire, 5x8 feet
5-foot wooden pole, 2 inches in diameter
pieces of wood to make brace for pole (and to fit inside bucket)
large stones or bricks (for weight)
dried plants, enough to completely cover the wire: filler for background, flowers for color

DIRECTIONS FOR TREE

The tree is built on a cone of chicken wire, with a wooden pole for support. These directions are for a 6-foot tree, but the tree may be any size you wish. Fill the wire with only a few different plant materials, or use a great variety—whichever you like. But in either case, you will need large quantities of filler.

To avoid moving finished tree, you may want to work in the room where tree will be placed. Spread newspapers on the floor before you begin.

1. Prepare base by making a wooden brace for the pole. Brace should fit into the bucket and hold the pole upright.
2. Place pole with brace inside bucket. Secure with stones or bricks.

3. Bend the 5-foot width of chicken wire into a double roll. Fit roll over pole so bottom end rests in bucket. Shape wire into a cone, tapering to a point at top, making height about 6 feet.
4. Begin building tree with one filler material, such as goldenrod. Insert stems into the chicken wire, and distribute evenly around tree, bottom to top. Use longest stems at the bottom, and keep the cone shape as you work. Use all the filler.
5. Add another filler material such as dusty miller or pearly everlasting.
6. Add other materials, one variety at a time. After tree is packed solid with fillers, add the colorful plants.
Note: Add strawflowers next to last. If tree is to be placed in a corner, you can save strawflowers for the front of the tree. Add baby's breath last.

Pine Tree Tablecloth

Let patchwork and calico add a homespun look to your holiday table. This tablecloth (pictured on p. 9, spread underneath the Christmas dinner), is done in red and green, using a patchwork pattern called Pine Tree. For buffet use, try adding a floor-length skirt of a solid color under the cloth to set it off.

Directions follow for making a rectangular tablecloth 66½x87½ inches, and for a 60-inch square cloth that can be used on a round table. The rectangular cloth may be enlarged by making outside strips wider, or by adding more pine tree blocks.

The pine tree blocks used to construct the cloth are 16 inches square, but they will

measure 15 inches square when set in the tablecloth. You can piece the blocks by hand or machine. Use ½-inch seam allowances, then trim to ⅛ inch after stitching. Work carefully and press as you go to keep the cloth flat, especially if it is left as one layer. If desired, the cloth can be lined with a cotton sheet blanket and machine-quilted.

Whether you use cotton or cotton-blend fabrics, it is best to shrink fabrics before you begin; just wash and dry the fabric as you would the finished tablecloth, but omit detergent.

DIRECTIONS FOR ONE PINE TREE BLOCK (16x16 INCHES)

Finished Pine Tree Block

Materials needed will vary according to the size of tablecloth you choose to make. These materials are listed separately with the directions for the rectangular and the square tablecloth.

1. See Fig. 1, noting that each square of the grid equals one inch on the finished patterns you will make. From poster board or cardboard, make the following patterns:
   A (3 inches square)
   B (a triangle, half of A)
   C (a triangle, one-half of a 9-inch square cut on the diagonal)

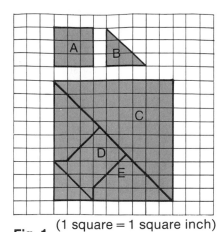

Fig. 1
Pattern for Pine Tree Block
(½-inch seam allowances
not shown)

    D (trunk of tree)
    E (area adjoining tree trunk)
2. For each pine tree block, trace patterns A-E on the back of fabric in pencil, add a ½-inch seam allowance around each pattern, and cut out as follows:

    A—2 pieces from green and
        white print fabric
    B—15 pieces from green and
        white print fabric and 14
        pieces from dark green
        fabric
    C—1 piece from dark green
        fabric
    D—1 piece from dark green
        fabric
    E—2 pieces from green print
        fabric, reversing one piece
        (see Fig 1)
3. Begin pine tree block by pinning a dark green B to a green print B along diagonal edges. Pin accurately on pencil lines and sew. Trim seam to ⅛ inch. Open to a square, and press seam to the dark side.
4. Repeat Step 3 to complete 13 more squares.
5. Place all pieces for one block in front of you, as in Fig. 2.
6. Sew together blocks in Row 1, pinning accurately at corners. Repeat for Row 2.
7. Sew together Row 1 and Row 2 to make Segment 1.
8. Sew together squares to

make Rows 3, 4 and 5, then complete Segment 2.
9. Sew E pieces to trunk D, clipping corners where necessary to press seam flat. Add green print B to bottom of trunk. Sew trunk to C to make Segment 3.
10. Pinning carefully at corners, sew Segment 2 to Segment 3. Attach to Segment 1.

![Fig. 2 diagram showing Segment 1, Segment 2, Segment 3, and Rows 1-5]

Fig. 2

MATERIALS FOR RECTANGULAR TABLE-CLOTH (66½x87½ INCHES)

1 yard dark green fabric, 45
    inches wide
1 yard green and white print fabric, 45 inches wide
4 yards red print fabric, 45
    inches wide
thread to coordinate with fabrics
poster board or cardboard for
    patterns
#2 pencil, well-sharpened, for
    tracing patterns on light fabric
yellow drawing pencil, for tracing patterns on dark fabric

DIRECTIONS FOR RECTANGULAR TABLE-CLOTH (66½x87½ INCHES)

1. Make six pine tree blocks (see preceding directions for making one block). Press well.
2. See Fig. 3. From poster

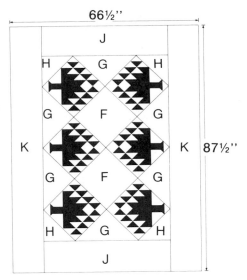

Fig. 3
Finished Rectangular Cloth

board or cardboard, make the following patterns:
    F (15 inches square)
    G (a triangle, half of F)
    H (a triangle, half of G)
3. Use pencil to trace these patterns on the back of red print fabric, add ½-inch seam allowances, and cut:
    F—2 pieces
    G—6 pieces
    H—4 pieces
4. See Fig. 3. Cut 2 strips J and two strips K as follows: From a 89½-inch length of red print fabric, measure across the 45-inch width, and cut three strips, each 13½ inches wide. Leave two of these strips 89½ inches long (K). Cut the third strip into 2 strips (J), each one 43½ inches long.
Note: This includes seam allowances and hems.
5. To assemble tablecloth, see Fig. 3; use ½-inch seam allowances. Sew blocks together for center section as follows: Join blocks and triangles along one diagonal line to form a row; then join the rows to complete the center. To add outside strips, first sew a short strip (J) to each
(continued on next page)

end. Then add the two long strips (K) to sides.

6. Hem, using 1-inch turnup.

MATERIALS FOR SQUARE TABLECLOTH (60x60 INCHES)

½ yard green and white print fabric, 45 inches wide
½ yard dark green fabric, 45 inches wide
2 yards red print fabric, 45 inches wide
thread to coordinate with fabrics
poster board or cardboard
#2 pencil
yellow drawing pencil

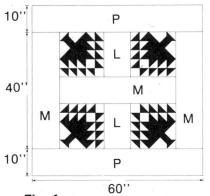

Fig. 4
Finished Square Cloth

DIRECTIONS FOR SQUARE TABLECLOTH (60x60 INCHES)

1. Make four pine tree blocks (see preceding directions for making one pine tree block). Press well.

2. See Fig. 4. From red print fabric, cut 7 strips as follows:

    L—2 strips, each 11x16 inches
    M—3 strips, each 11x41 inches
    P—2 strips, each 11x61 inches

Note: This includes seam allowances and hems.

3. Assemble blocks and strips, following Fig. 4; use ½-inch seam allowances. Complete center square, then add end

strips (M). Last, add long strips (P).

4. Hem, using ½-inch turnup.

Poinsettia Napkin Rings

The poinsettia napkin rings (see illustration, p. 9) are inspired by another patchwork pattern. We used them with the patchwork tablecloth, but they also look smashing on a white cloth with white napkins—just the right touch for a festive meal.

MATERIALS FOR 8 NAPKIN RINGS

poster board (or cardboard) for patterns
¼ yard green fabric, 45 inches wide
⅜ yard red fabric, 45 inches wide
⅛ yard red and yellow print fabric (predominantly yellow), 45 inches wide
thread to match fabrics

DIRECTIONS FOR EACH NAPKIN RING

1. On poster board or cardboard, copy leaf and petal patterns.

2. Using leaf pattern, trace four leaves in pencil on wrong side of green fabric; add at least ¼ inch for seam allowance. **Note:** When tracing diamond shapes, keep two edges of the pattern on the straight grain of the fabric. Do this by placing one side of the diamond parallel to the selvage.

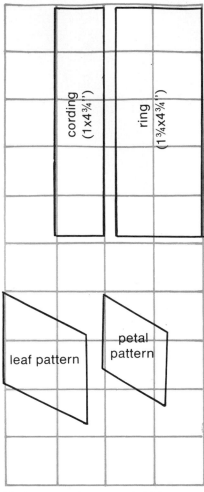

(1 square = 1 square inch)

3. On green fabric, mark rectangle for ring (seam allowance is included in measurement).

4. Using petal pattern, trace eight petals in pencil on wrong side of red fabric; add at least ¼ inch all around for seam allowance.

5. On print fabric, measure strip for cording (the seam allowance is included).

6. Cut out fabric pieces.

7. Place two leaf pieces right sides together, and pin through drawn lines at each point. Stitch along drawn lines, leaving a ½-inch opening on one side. Turn leaf to right side and close opening with blind stitches. Repeat to make second leaf.

8. Place two petal pieces, right sides together, and pin and
(continued on p. 108)

Cornhusk Craft

The revival of old-time crafts has made cornhusk dolls popular once again. The dolls shown here, like those made by Native Americans many years ago, have faces without features—adding features was thought to bring bad luck. The hair for these dolls was fashioned from corn silk, but you could substitute yarn.

Cornhusks also can be made into simple flowers (shown here arranged with tiny dried flowers), seven-pointed stars and angels with fluffy tutus.

You can use the natural colors of the husks, or dye them any color you wish. Both methods are illustrated by the dolls with their full skirts, aprons, pinafore tops and puffed sleeves.

These dolls and ornaments were made from the husks of field corn taken after the first frost, meaning that the husks were dry and loosened from the ears. Husks of sweet corn must be dried. You also can buy cornhusks at some craft stores.

Working with cornhusks is time-consuming and somewhat messy. In most cases, the husks must be wet so that they are pliable. Directions are given for all the items pictured, but you'll find that the dolls and angels you make will be unique. It seems that everyone develops an individual "cornhusk style." You'll also find that the first doll is the hardest: the second one should be easier to assemble—and much better looking.

GENERAL INFORMATION

To dye husks, use 1 tsp. fabric dye in ½ gal. hot water. Soak husks until you get the color you want; remember that the color will be lighter when dry. Rinse dyed husks as you would fabric, then place on newspaper to dry.

When working with husks, (either natural or dyed), soak them 10 to 15 minutes in warm water to make them pliable.

Cornhusks you peel off the corn yourself will have a triangular shape, tapering to a point at one end. Husks you buy in a package may be shorter and cut straight across. If you buy husks, you can substitute yarn for corn silk to make hair for the angel and doll.

An optional finish for any cornhusk craft is an acrylic spray. This adds a protective coating and helps keep items clean. Apply only after items are completely dry.

Angel

The hands and skirt are shredded and curled for a fluffy look. Finished angel will be 3½ inches tall and 2½ inches wide.

MATERIALS

cornhusks, left natural, from
    about 2 ears of corn
corn silk from 1 ear of corn
Styrofoam ball, 1-inch diameter
string
standard pipe cleaner
sewing needle
brown thread
thin gold string
thin gold wire
white glue

DIRECTIONS

1. For head and body, use two large pieces of husks, each 3 inches wide and 5 or 6 inches long. Place one piece on top of the other.
2. Tear about 30 cornhusk strips, each ¼ inch wide and the length of the large husks. Center 15 strips on both front and back of the large husks (Fig. 1).

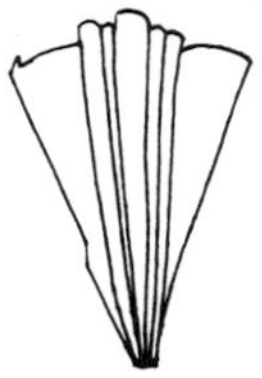

Fig. 1

3. Tie 1 inch from top, and trim top to form a half round (Fig. 2).

Fig. 2

4. Turn husks upside down; separate the two large husks, and curve them down over the half round. Place the Styrofoam ball inside the husks, against the half round (Fig. 3). Press husks around ball, and tie tightly under ball (for neck).

Fig. 3

5. For arms, cut a 3x4-inch piece of husk. Center a 3-inch length of pipe cleaner along the long edge of husk and roll up. Tie roll at ends of pipe cleaner, leaving at least ¼ inch to form hands.
6. With needle, shred ends (hands).
7. Place arm roll behind the head, just below neck (Fig. 4). To tie, take string under arm and over opposite shoulder, making a crisscross.

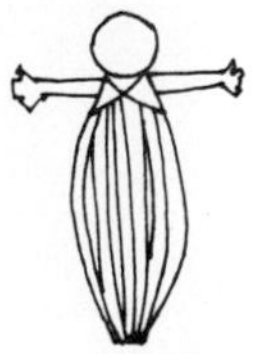

Fig. 4

8. To make pinafore top, use a 3x5-inch piece of husk. Fold the 3-inch width to make a strip ½ inch wide. Repeat to make a second strip.
9. Place one folded strip over each shoulder, crossing strips at the waist, front and back. Tie tightly at waist (Fig. 5).

Fig. 5

10. With a sewing needle, shred the skirt below the waist as you did the hands. Cut across the bottom of the skirt to make it even; leave it 3 or 4 inches long.
11. Place angel upside down in small juice glass or other container, with skirt above rim. Let dry overnight; as skirt dries, it will curl.
12. For hair, you can use wet or dry corn silk. Place silk flat and tie with brown thread at middle to form a part. Put glue on angel's head; arrange corn silk on head with part at the top. Tie a pony tail behind neck (Fig. 6), then bring tail up to form a bun on the back of the head. Tuck ends of silk and string inside bun at top, and glue.

Fig. 6

13. To hang, make loop of gold string. Tuck ends in bun at top of head, and glue to hold.

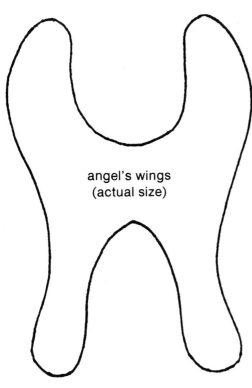

angel's wings
(actual size)

14. To make halo, braid thin gold wire, place on top of head and glue.

15. Add wings last. Copy pattern for angel wings and cut them from a large piece of husk. Glue to back of angel.

Doll

The finished doll will be about 6½ inches tall. You can make a slimmer skirt by using fewer husks. For a little girl doll, shorten both the length of arm piece and the length of skirt by 1 inch, and use a smaller Styrofoam ball for head.

If you dye husks to make these dolls, you can dye extra husks to make matching flowers. You can also outfit each doll with a small basket, available at craft stores, dyed to match the doll and filled with dried flowers.

MATERIALS

cornhusks from about 4 ears of corn
corn silk from one ear of corn
string
Styrofoam ball, 1 inch diameter
standard pipe cleaner
bobby pins or hair clips
drinking glass

DIRECTIONS

1. For head and body, use 2 large pieces of husks, each 3 inches wide and 5 or 6 inches long. Place one piece on top of the other.

2. Tear about 30 cornhusk strips, each ¼ inch wide and the length of the large husks. Center 15 strips on both front and back of the large husks (Fig. 1).

Fig. 1

3. Tie 1 inch from top, and trim top to form a half round (Fig. 2).

Fig. 2

4. Turn husks upside down; separate the two large husks, and curve them down over the half round. Place the Styrofoam ball inside the husks, against the half round (Fig. 3). Press husks around ball, and tie tightly under ball (for neck).

5. For arms, cut a 3x5½-inch piece of husk. Center a 5-inch length of pipe cleaner along the long edge of husk and roll up. Tie tightly ¼ inch from each end (at wrist).

Fig. 3

6. To make full sleeves, cut a 3½-inch square from husk. Place husk on arm so it extends out over hand, overlapping arm by only ¾ inch. Gather husk around arm and tie tightly over string at wrist (Fig. 4). Pull husk

Fig. 4

back over the arm and tie at center of arm (Fig. 5). Repeat to make sleeve on other side.

Fig. 5

7. Place arms behind head and tie tightly (see Fig. 6).

Fig. 6

8. To make pinafore top, take a 3x5-inch piece of husk. Fold the 3-inch width to make a strip ½ inch wide. Repeat to make a second strip.

9. Place one folded strip over each shoulder, crossing strips at the waist, front and back. Tie tightly at waist (Fig. 7).

Fig. 7

(continued on p. 108)

Clothespin Dolls

To make these dolls, you'll need some of those old-fashioned wooden clothespins. The free-standing or hanging angel, Santa and soldiers pictured here take advantage of the clothespin's natural shape; cork balls are used as heads to give them extra height. Patterns are included on p. 109.

Angel

MATERIALS

1 wooden clothespin
¾-inch cork ball
white glue
blue felt-tipped pen
1 king-sized gold pipe cleaner (or 2⅛ inches of gold yarn)
1 aluminum pipe cleaner (or 3¼ inches of thin wire)
9-inch square of gold construction paper
12 inches of blue yarn or cord
silver decorator tape, ½ inch wide (or aluminum foil)
6-inch square white doily
8 inches of yellow thread

DIRECTIONS

1. Glue cork ball to the top of clothespin. Draw eyes on cork with pen.
2. To make hair, cut gold pipe cleaner (or gold yarn) and glue to head. To make halo, bend one end of aluminum pipe cleaner or wire into a circle and push other end into cork head.
3. To make dress, draw an 8¾-inch circle on gold paper. In the center draw another circle ¾ inch in diameter (see diagram on p. 109). Dress will be one-third of the large circle (shaded area). Mark off large circle into thirds; then draw line to connect two of the division points with center of circle.
4. Cut out dress (shaded area in diagram). Wrap dress around bottom of clothespin head and glue together to make a cone.

70

Measure enough yarn or cord to completely encircle bottom of dress; cut and glue to dress.

5. To make collar, cut ½-inch wide strip of silver tape or foil. Wrap around bottom of angel's head. Use blue yarn or cord to trim by gluing to top of collar.

6. Trace wing pattern on white doily folded in half. Cut out and glue to back of collar.

7. To hang doll, knot thread to make loop and tie to neck.

Santa

This clothespin Santa has jiggly eyes that look right at you to see if you've been "naughty or nice." You can buy doll eyes in several sizes at most craft or hobby shops.

MATERIALS

1 wooden clothespin
¾-inch cork ball
white glue
red felt, 5¾x8¾ inches
silver decorator tape, ½ inch wide (or aluminum foil)
3 balls of cotton
tracing paper
2 (¼-inch) doll eyes (or felt-tipped pen)
8 inches of red thread

DIRECTIONS

1. Glue cork ball to top of clothespin.
2. To make trousers, measure and cut a felt piece to fit neatly around each clothespin leg. Felt should overlap slightly. Glue to each leg. Wrap a ½-inch wide strip of silver tape or foil around bottom of each leg; glue.
3. To make jacket, measure and cut felt strip to fit neatly around body. Felt should overlap slight-

ly. Glue in place.
4. To make arms, cut 2 pieces of felt 1½x1⅝ inches. (Arm length is 1½ inches.) Roll each piece tightly and secure with glue. Glue to body so that arms just touch cork head.
5. To make hands, divide a cotton ball into 2 tiny balls and glue to arms.
6. To make belt, glue tape or foil around top of legs. To make buckle, cut a ⅜-inch square of felt and a ⅛-inch square of tape or foil. Glue tape or foil to felt; glue felt to belt.
7. Trace hat pattern on tracing paper; pin to red felt and cut out. Glue hat together to form cone. Divide a cotton ball in half. Roll a thin piece of cotton for brim and glue to hat. Snip off tip of hat. Roll a small cotton ball and glue to top of hat. Glue hat to head.
8. Form beard from cotton ball; glue around face, leaving room for eyes and nose. Glue doll eyes to head or draw eyes with pen. Cut ¼-inch circle from felt for nose; glue to face.
9. To hang doll, knot red thread to make loop and stitch or pin to back of Santa.

Soldier

MATERIALS

1 wooden clothespin
¾-inch cork ball
white glue
magenta felt, 5¾x8¾ inches
gold decorator tape, ½ inch wide (or gold foil, 3x5 inches)
10 inches of yellow embroidery cotton
cotton ball
2 (¼-inch) doll eyes (or felt-tipped pen)
8 inches of red thread

DIRECTIONS

1. Glue cork ball to top of clothespin.
2. To make trousers, measure and cut a felt piece to fit neatly around each clothespin leg. Felt should overlap slightly. Glue to each leg. Wrap a ½-inch-wide strip of gold tape or foil around bottom of each leg; glue.
3. Measure and cut felt strip to fit neatly around body. Felt should overlap slightly. Glue in place. To make collar, cut a ¼-inch-wide strip of gold tape or foil and wrap around clothespin at base of head; glue. To make belt, wrap ½-inch-wide strip of tape or foil around top of legs; glue.
4. Measure and cut two thin strips of gold tape or foil the length of each leg; glue to outside of each leg.
5. To make arms, cut 2 squares of felt 1½x1½ inches. Roll tightly and secure with glue. Glue to body.
6. To make hands, divide a cotton ball into 2 tiny balls and glue to arms.
7. To decorate jacket, cut an 8-inch length of embroidery cotton in half. Glue end of one half to right top of belt, wrap over opposite shoulder and glue in back at right top of belt. Trim. Repeat with other half, beginning at left.
8. To make hat, cut felt piece ¾x2½ inches. Roll into a cylinder to fit head; overlap and glue. Roll a small ball of cotton and place in top of hat. Cut a ⅝-inch length of embroidery cotton for hat strap; glue to hat. Glue hat to head, placing strap carefully under chin.
9. Glue doll eyes to head, or draw eyes. Cut tiny felt triangle for nose and glue to face.
10. To hang doll, knot red thread to make loop and stitch or pin to back of soldier.

CHAPTER 5

THE JOY OF GIVING

One of the best things about Christmas is the opportunity it offers to plan a whole season full of surprises: a tin of homemade candy for a neighbor; a limited edition of original Christmas cards for a close circle of friends; a needlepoint pillow for a daughter-in-law.

Recipes for cookies, candy and other food gifts are given on pages 18-30; in this chapter are ideas and instructions for greeting cards, needlework projects, photograph framing and holiday invitations. There are many more possibilities, of course, just waiting to be discovered: for clues to finding the perfect gift, turn to page 95.

Greetings to Make and Mail

Christmas cards bring cheer throughout the season, and these five designs not only carry your greetings, but also become stand-up decorations when they reach their destinations.

Any child would love the Santa or the yellow house with candles glowing in the windows—but then, so would an adult. These two designs, as well as the pink-and-gold crown, have their own matching envelopes.

The Christmas tree and the bell, on the other hand, are self-contained: As the cards are opened, the designs pop out.

Be sure to keep your messages brief and write them in places where they won't detract from the designs. If you use a felt-tipped pen, be careful not to let the ink bleed through the paper.

For directions and patterns, turn to p.110.

Christmas greetings are even more personal when they're penned on a handcrafted card. The house, crown and Santa designs have their own matching envelopes; the tree and bell are self-contained.

The Gift That's Picture-Perfect

For proud parents, grandparents and people in love, a photograph of the object of one's affections has always been a treasured gift.

Here are ways to enhance the enjoyment of photographs by displaying them in novel settings. Imagine the nostalgic appeal of a keepsake clock, with each hour marked by a photograph of your son in his years from one to twelve, or a romantic photograph of your daughter playing a scene from her high school play, woven into a wall hanging.

These arrangements are made with items familiar to needleworkers and decoupage and macrame enthusiasts. Carpentry is minimal, and basic materials are available at most craft shops.

Woven Frame

Use your imagination to weave your own design above and below the photo centered in this loom, or follow directions given for the samples.

MATERIALS

1   5x7-inch unfinished wood frame, painted white
4   lengths of ½-inch balsa wood: 2 (18-inch) lengths and 2 (12-inch) lengths, painted white
1   skein white knitting yarn
crochet hook (any size)
clear craft glue
1   5x7-inch photo
14 upholstery nails
4   1-inch finishing nails
5   yards fine sturdy macrame cord, navy
5   yards 5mm acrylic macrame cord, white
1   yard acrylic roving, navy
1   yard acrylic roving, white
1   sawtooth picture hanger

DIRECTIONS

1. Wrap frame and all 4 balsa pieces with white yarn. To wrap frame, first wrap each edge or side lengthwise, then wrap yarn around each side crosswise (see Fig. 1). Trim ends and pull back under work, using a crochet hook.

2. Spread glue on back of wrapped frame and place photo against it, right side of photo facing through frame. (If photo is not large enough to glue securely to back of frame, cut a piece of cardboard a little larger than photo and attach to back of photo, then glue cardboard to frame.) Allow to dry.

3. Pound the upholstery nails through photo into frame from back side, 7 along the top edge of frame and 7 along the bottom, beginning ½ inch from each corner of frame and spacing evenly between nails. Each nail should be secure in the wood, but extend enough for yarn to be wrapped around it.

4. Connect balsa wood pieces to form a rectangle, placing longer pieces (side pieces) on top of shorter pieces (top and bottom pieces), with 1½ inches of each piece extending beyond joinings. Connect by nailing with finishing nails. Add a coat of glue for extra support.

5. Position picture frame in center of rectangle and lace into place, beginning along top edge, by tying one end of sturdy navy cord to one top end nail, drawing it up and around top balsa piece in a larkshead knot (see Fig. 2), bringing it down around same nail, then drawing it over to the second nail, wrapping it around, drawing it up and around top balsa piece in a larkshead knot, continuing across top (see Fig. 3). Tie cord end around last nail and trim. Repeat procedure on bottom edge.

6. Add weaving to top and bottom of frame. (Directions for making weaving follow.)

7. Attach sawtooth picture hanger to center back of top balsa bar.

WEAVING

1. Working over a pair of navy cords, then under a pair, finger-weave 4 rows of white macrame cord across top of navy cords next to top balsa piece.

2. Split the yard of navy roving into 4 sections lengthwise and weave 1 of the sections beneath the 4 rows of white cord in the same manner until it runs out.

3. Weave 4 rows of white macrame cord beneath navy roving.

4. Split the yard of white roving into 4 lengthwise sections and use 1 section to weave beneath the white cord until it runs out.

5. Weave 4 rows of white macrame cord beneath white roving.

6. Use another section of navy roving to weave beneath white macrame cord until it runs out.

7. Trim all cord and roving ends on back and weave into back of work, using a crochet hook.

8. Turn work upside down and repeat weaving at bottom.

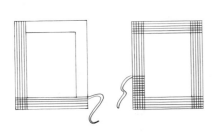

Fig. 1

Fig. 2

Fig. 3

Keepsake Clock

Directions are given for a clock 12 inches in diameter, but one much larger could be made. Hobby clock components are designed to fit all sizes.

(continued on next page)

MATERIALS

12 (1½-inch) metal macrame rings

12 small photos of child from age 1 to 12

18 yards knitting yarn, beige crochet hook

1 round or octagonal wood plaque for decoupage, 11 or 12 inches in diameter, ¼ inch thick, stained and drilled in center with ¼-inch hole (or see clock component directions for exact size of hole)

2 pkgs. transfer type and numbers (or stencil card and ink)

1 set hobby clock components, battery-operated

instant decoupage liquid

clear craft glue

DIRECTIONS

1. Place metal ring over each photo so that face is centered inside. Trace around outside of ring with pencil and cut photo along pencil line.

2. Cut yarn into 12 (1½-yard) lengths and cover each ring with yarn by tying half hitches all around. Trim the excess cord and pull the ends into the work, using a crochet hook. Be sure rings cover edges of photos; trim photos if needed.

3. Place photos around wood plaque in clockwise fashion, each photo about ½ inch from edge. (Place photo of 1-year-old in 1 o'clock position and work clockwise.) Outline each photo lightly with pencil to mark position, then glue in place.

4. Measure and mark positions for numbers around the clock, with each number about ½ inch from the corresponding photo. Place numbers on clock with transfer type, or stencil.

5. Measure and mark center for child's name above hole (same position as "Chris" in photo) and the word "at" below. Allow plenty of room for center of clock components. Letter the child's name and the word "at" with transfer type or stencil.

6. Spread entire clock face, including lettering, numbers and photos, with a coat of decoupage liquid. Allow to dry thoroughly and repeat.

7. Spread craft glue on one side of each wrapped ring and center a ring over each photo. Remove excess glue; let dry overnight.

8. Attach clock components to center hole, following manufacturer's directions.

Pinup Board

This display may be made with a variety of frames chosen to suit the photos and mounted on
(continued on p. 116)

A Very Special Invitation

By ADELAIDE ALTMAN

People are pushovers for holiday parties. And why not? They hold the promise of cheery greetings from friends old and new, merry tales of Christmases past and present, and fabulous foods making once-a-year appearances.

Small wonder that holiday hosts and hostesses plan early to make each year's gatherings more festive than ever. And what better place to start than at the very beginning: Let your invitations become a part of the festivities by sending messages so warm and personal your guests will never forget them.

Finding the right invitation, however, may present a problem. The ready-made, fill-in-your-name varieties usually don't convey a personal touch. And custom-printed styles ordinarily are expensive. Why not do it yourself?

Here are some ideas to stir your imagination.

Send a small gift instead of a card: Tie a tag to it announcing the date, time and place of your party, then wrap it in a nest of bright tissue within a box. An inexpensive mailing carton will do, but tie it with pretty string.

What you enclose is limited only by your time and imagination. (You should, however, select something lightweight to keep postage costs within reason.) Here are a few examples.

Send a gift of nature:

● A spray of holly festively tied with bright ribbon and a card reading, "We've decked the halls. Join us!"

● A beautiful pine cone, with card saying, "We pine for you!"

• An acorn doll with a Christmas ribbon around its waist and card that reads, "Be a doll and join us for brunch."

Have the children look for acorns that have their "hats" still intact. (It's a good idea to spray with an insecticide lest you later discover you mailed wormy greetings!) Select one acorn with a "hat" for the head, then attach two large acorns to represent the upper torso and lower torso. This is easily done by inserting pieces of round wooden toothpicks. You may need to start the holes with an awl or some other pointed instrument. Then add two smaller acorns for each arm and three for each leg, graduating in size and ending with small acorns, with the "hats" facing down to form "shoes." Presto! A doll worthy to beckon guests to a holiday feast.

Or send a gift of food:
• A gingerbread man with a message to "Run, run as fast as you can to our Christmas party."
• A smiley-faced, over-sized cookie urging, "Smile awhile with us."
• A popcorn ball nestled in a box with the promise, "Things will be popping at our house."
• A candy cane or small sack of Christmas candies plus an invitation to "Be sweet and join us at our holiday brunch."

Or send a gift of the season:
• A bell or two with a summons to "Jingle, jingle, come and mingle!"
• A toy train or soldier whistling the message, "Come play with us!"
• A mini-Santa cut out of felt, decorated with simple embroidery and bringing the gay greeting, "There's a pack of Christmas fun at our house." This could become a tree ornament reminding your friends of your thoughtfulness.
• A Christmas bauble tagged, "Have a ball at our house."
• A pretty angel sweetly saying, "Be an angel: Come to our party."

Or send a gift that holds special meaning:
• A key to say, "Open house." Gather some discarded keys, or have new ones made by your local locksmith or hardware store. You might buy costume jewelry in the shape of decorative keys, or cut king-sized keys out of cardboard and sheath them in colored foil.
• A symbol that fits your image. Farm families might choose a miniature lamb ("Be a lamb and come to our party") or a tiny rooster ("Come crow with us!"). Make your own of felt and embroidery,

or look for miniatures in gift shops, toy stores or the notions sections of fabric stores.

Or just send a cheerful thought:
You can make many original party invitations with a handcrafted, show-that-you-care appearance. Try one of these:
• Affix a photo of your invited guest to an unprinted Christmas folder, and in red or green ink write your own message, "YOU are invited . . . ." Use snapshots of your friends that have been taken earlier in the year—at the beach or during a visit.
• In your prettiest handwriting, write your invitation on plain or colored 8½x11-inch sheets of paper. This size, when folded in thirds, fits neatly into standard business envelopes, eliminating the problem and expense of finding special envelopes.

Embellish by attaching real holly leaves outlined with red felt-tipped pen. Or add tinsel attached with double-faced tape, leaving some of it loose to spill out when the invitation is opened.
• Spatter-print some leaf designs. This is great fun to do and so easy that your little ones can help. You'll need some large, well-shaped leaves such as oak, maple, poinsettia or whatever is available in your climate. Artificial leaves will do if nothing else is on hand. You'll also need sheets of 8½x11-inch bond or parchment paper; straight pins; two or three colors of washable ink or watercolor mixture; lots of old newspapers to catch the dribbles and several old toothbrushes.

Spread out the newspapers on a flat surface and place single sheets of your paper on top. Next, fasten several leaves in place on each sheet (you can work out your own design) with the pins inserted on a slant. Then very lightly dip the brush into the color, using one brush per color. Gently rub your thumb across the bristles to make little spatters or dots of color over the leaves and sheets. When the first color is dry, repeat with the second and third colors. Allow each to dry. Then remove the pins and lift off the leaves. The unspattered impressions of the leaves will give you the space to write your invitation.

Now roll up each invitation as you would a diploma, tie it with a ribbon and post it in a mailing tube.

Other easy holiday touches are figures cut from colored felt or construction paper, or snowflakes made from paper doilies and outlined in color.

Is you imagination beginning to stir? You can design something new and different that carries your own trademark. Whatever you choose to send, your guests will know that a very special party awaits them—by invitation.

Accessories that Travel in Style

A carryall makes a perfect present for someone who's always on the move. The matching garment bag and duffel bag are tailored for practicality, and when they travel as a team, the garment bag and duffel bag hold just enough for a weekend visit. Use strong, washable fabric, and they'll withstand more tossing around than many plastic bags you can buy.

Garment Bag

MATERIALS

Bag may be made in several lengths, and the length you decide upon will determine the amount of material required. To hold suit coats and jackets, you'll need a finished bag about 40 inches long—longer for dresses.

zipper, 40 inches long (or length of finished bag)
fabric, 45 inches wide and 1 inch longer than zipper (to provide a ½-inch seam allowance at both top and bottom)

DIRECTIONS

1. Shrink zipper and fabric by washing and drying as you would finished bag, but omit detergent. Cut through selvages on edges of fabric, then turn under and press flat so that fabric does not pucker.

2. Place zipper and fabric right side up. On fabric, mark off a ½-inch seam allowance for top of bag. Lay a folded edge of fabric over zipper tape and stitch (keeping zipper exposed). Use two rows of straight stitching or a row of zigzag stitching to keep zipper edges flat and to reinforce zipper. Repeat on other side of fabric and zipper.

3. Turn bag wrong side out and center zipper on one side. Sew a ½-inch seam along bottom edge.

4. At top edge, make a curve (see Fig. 1). Measure down one side 6½ inches from the corner. Use a hanger as a guide and mark a curve, sloping from center of bag. Cut along the line, then stitch, using a ½-inch seam allowance. Repeat to make curve on other side of bag.

5. Reinforce stitching at top and bottom of zipper. Turn right side out and press.

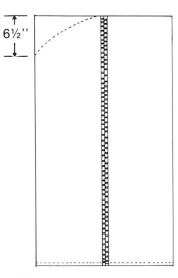

Fig. 1 Garment Bag

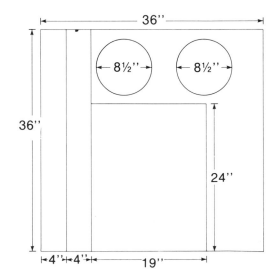

Fig. 2 Duffel Bag

Duffel Bag

MATERIALS

1 yard sturdy fabric, 36 or 44
   inches wide; thread to match
1 (18-inch) zipper

DIRECTIONS

1. Shrink fabric and zipper. See Fig. 2, and cut two strips of fabric 4x36 inches. Cut one 19x24-inch rectangle, and two 8½-inch circles.

2. To make handle, sew the two strips together to make one continuous strip (a circle), using ½-inch seam allowances.

3. Fold raw edges to center of strip, wrong sides together. Fold in half again and press. Stitch together to make a 1x70-inch circular strip.

4. To assemble bag, use rectangular section of fabric and zipper. Line up one 19-inch edge of fabric with one edge of zipper, right sides together. (Place zipper face down on fabric.) Stitch ¼ inch from edge. Repeat, stitching along 19-inch edge of fabric to other edge of zipper.

5. Turn to right side and press fabric away from zipper. Topstitch fabric close to zipper. (This holds zipper away from fabric and reinforces seam.)

6. Attach handle by placing the two seams of the continuous strip at center of bottom of bag, and 4 inches from the outside edges. Sew each side of strip to bag up to within 3 inches from the zipper. Stitch crosses at this point to reinforce. (Straps come up on each side of bag but do not cross over zipper.)

7. Turn to wrong side. Attach circles to end of bag, using ½-inch seam allowances. Double-stitch across ends of zipper.

8. Turn right side out.

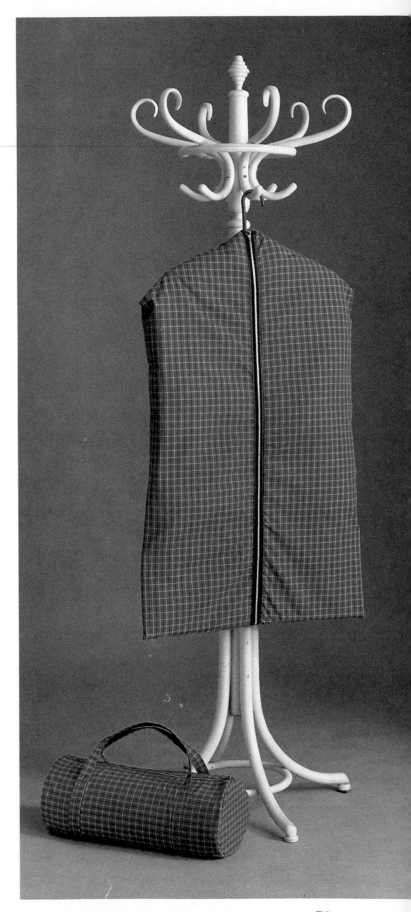

Appliqué for Tots and Teens

Here are four ways to use applique to make a gift that's both personal and practical: a teenager's T-shirt, a nightshirt, a bib and a baby's undershirt.

The Sunshine Shirt, a standard T-shirt brightened with fabric scraps and embroidery, will bring a burst of cheer to any cloudy day.

The Slumber Shirt is made for a girl whose heart belongs to Daddy—and whose shirts sometimes belong to him, too. This nightshirt is casual and feminine, and it's made from one of the most comfortable fabrics of all—beneath the ribbon and lace is a man's undershirt.

The Baby Bib is made from a terry cloth hand towel to fit the toddler who's the apple of your eye, and the three baby T-shirts make appealing, inexpensive gifts for any new baby or toddler. Patterns are included on p. 117.

Sunshine Shirt

The T-shirt you use to make this shirt may be made or purchased. (Directions are not given for making T-shirt.) The sun applique looks attractive on a shirt of almost any color.

MATERIALS

girl's or woman's T-shirt
scraps of fabric: yellow print, orange print and polka dot
press-on interfacing
press-on bonding fabric (optional)
orange thread
black embroidery thread

DIRECTIONS

(For directions on how to enlarge a pattern, see p. 97. For directions on how to make embroidery stitches, see p. 98.)

1. Prewash and dry shirt.
2. Press interfacing onto back of fabric scraps.
3. Enlarge sun ray patterns and transfer to yellow and orange print fabric scraps, alternating colors. Cut out. Trace sun center pattern and transfer to yellow or orange polka dot fabric (whichever looks best on your shirt). Cut out. Trace cheek patterns and transfer to fabric. (Using a fabric that contrasts with sun face is not necessary, but adds a nice touch.) Cut out. Position on face and machine-stitch into place, using a zigzag stitch.
4. Place T-shirt on ironing board. Center sunshine design close to neckline of shirt. Make sure ends of rays are underneath the center face circle. Attach with press-on bonding (cut the same shape as the design) or baste.
5. Adjust sewing machine for satin stitch with stitch width on widest zigzag pattern.
6. Satin-stitch applique to T-shirt. Sew around sun face first, then attach rays.
7. Embroider face onto sun with black embroidery thread. Use stem stitch for face, and satin-stitch to fill in centers of eyes. Press.

Slumber Shirt

To guarantee a good fit, you'll need to know the upper arm measurement of the girl who'll be wearing this shirt.

MATERIALS

The trim shown is a purchased embroidered ruffle with a strip of red and white checked fabric down the center, but any lace trim could be used.

man's undershirt, large
3 yards double-sided lace trim or embroidered lace ruffle; thread to match
2 lengths of ½-inch elastic, each ½ inch longer than upper arm measurement
fabric scraps; thread to match
white thread
press-on interfacing
½ yard narrow satin ribbon

DIRECTIONS

(For directions on how to enlarge a pattern, see p. 97.)
1. Prewash and dry shirt.
2. Place trim down center front of shirt; stitch both sides.
3. Place trim around neck, below ribbing and around bottom of shirt. Stitch both sides.
4. Cut elastic. Turn up hem of each sleeve of shirt and stitch to make a casing; run a length of elastic through each casing and stitch together. Stitch casings closed.
5. Press interfacing onto back of fabric scraps.
6. Enlarge heart applique patterns and transfer onto fabric scraps. Cut out.
7. Adjust sewing machine for satin stitch with stitch width on widest zigzag pattern. Attach appliques, with hearts overlapping, to shoulder of shirt, using satin stitch. Press.

Baby Bib

This bib goes on and off easily and can't come untied because it slips over the head. It's made from a fingertip terry towel, fabric applique and neckline ribbing. Use fabric scraps to applique a design, or cut a design from a printed fabric.

MATERIALS

fingertip terry cloth towel, 11x18 inches (including fringe)
knitted ribbing, 3 inches wide (along the ribs) and 15 inches long (across the ribs); thread to match
fabric for applique; thread to match
press-on bonding (optional)

DIRECTIONS

For directions on how to enlarge a pattern, see p. 97.)
1. Enlarge the half-circle pattern for neckline. Fold down the

(continued on p. 116)

Double Cross-Stitch Pillows

The handsome pillows pictured here are worked with only one stitch, the double cross-stitch. It's an easy stitch to learn, and once you've mastered it you'll enjoy creating your own designs.

Directions for making the double cross-stitch and patterns for these pillows follow. Make the pillows in the colors shown, or design your own color combinations. If you do decide on a new color scheme, it's a good idea to try a corner of the pattern first to see how the colors you've chosen suit the pattern.

The double cross-stitch may be used to make chair seats, footstool covers and even tote bags as well as pillow tops.

DIRECTIONS FOR USING DOUBLE CROSS-STITCH

1. Each stitch uses a square of nine meshes or holes: three vertically and three horizontally. Work the first cross diagonally.
2. Work the second cross horizontally and vertically. The last strand of yarn on all stitches should run in the same direction, as in regular cross-stitch. However, it makes no difference which diagonal stitch goes in first, so to conserve yarn, begin next stitch at the corner nearest the end of the previous stitch.

Note: Adjoining stitches in finished work will share the meshes between them; so adjoining stitches use five meshes in a row instead of six.

MATERIALS

The pillows shown were worked on 7-mesh Penelope canvas. (The number indicates holes, or meshes, per inch.)

The size of canvas and amount of other materials needed to make each pillow are given with the individual patterns on pp. 117-118.

A double strand of wool tapestry yarn is used throughout the pillow and will cover the canvas. This yarn is available at needlework shops.

Yarn colors are based on the original pillows and are identified on individual patterns by symbols.

In our patterns, each square represents one complete stitch, and the symbol in each square indicates the color of yarn used. To help you follow the pattern more easily, you may want to lightly color the pattern to correspond with each color of yarn you use.

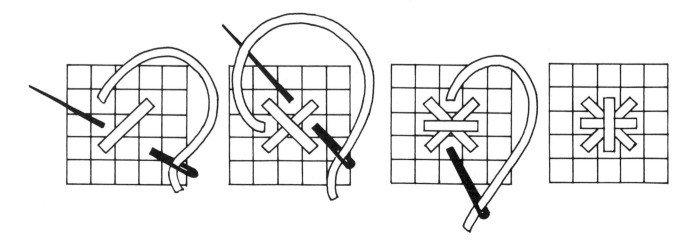

One easy needlework stitch was used to make these three pillows. Patterns are included on pp. 117-118.

GENERAL DIRECTIONS

(Patterns are included on pp. 117-118.)

1. Cover edge of canvas with masking tape, or machine-stitch with zigzag stitches to prevent raveling.

2. Begin working the pattern on the canvas, leaving a 1½-inch border on all sides (this has been allowed in the canvas measurement). Work the pattern in a double cross-stitch. Use a double strand of yarn and keep your work firm but not tight.

3. It is not necessary to work in rows, and it is easier to work all the stitches of one color in one area at a time. Do not tie knots at the start or finish of a strand of yarn. Instead, pull the ends through stitches on the wrong side of work to secure.

4. When pattern is completed, use your machine to zigzag-stitch around the outside, as close to the yarn as possible. Then trim away extra canvas close to the stitching line, leaving a ½-inch seam allowance.

5. Pin backing fabric to canvas, right sides together, and with edges of backing extending outside edges of canvas. Machine-stitch around edges, leaving a portion of one seam open for turning. For even lines, stitch around the pillow in the center of the first row of stitches on the canvas. Cut away corners of backing fabric only; trim seams of backing fabric to ½ inch.

6. Turn pillow to right side. Stuff with fiberfill and close opening with hand-stitches.

(continued on p. 117)

CHAPTER 6

CHRISTMAS IS FOR CHILDREN

For a child, Christmas is the high point of the year: the decorations, the special treats, the secret planning and whispering behind closed doors, the anticipation of a visit from Old St. Nick— all these things build up to a level of excitement and suspense that is almost too much for a child to bear. The excitement of children at Christmas time is contagious, causing each of us to remember our own feelings as a child. It's no wonder that often our fondest holiday memories are those of our own childhood, or of a Christmas we've shared with children.

But caught up with the busy preparations of the season, we may find ourselves saying much too often, "Don't touch that" or "I have to get this finished, so play by yourself for a while." It's easy to forget, when you're busy, that Christmas is for children.

Children want to be included in the preparations. They like to help decorate the tree and they like to make Christmas gifts, too. So perhaps the best gift you can give a child at Christmas is the gift of your time. By themselves, or with your help, children can make decorations and hanging ornaments from pine cones and aluminum foil. They'll be proud of being able to give dried-flower terrariums or batik handkerchiefs they've made themselves, and this chapter tells how.

Of course, we can't forget that children need to receive presents, too. So in this chapter you'll also find directions for making several gifts of clothing and toys. Any little girl will find it hard to resist Long-legged Linda, pictured at right. And we think you yourself will find it hard to resist giving gifts like these—gifts of your hands, your time and your love—to make this Christmas special for children.

Long-legged Linda

Measuring 24 inches tall, with movable arms and legs, this doll is a perky companion for any little girl. Perched on a chair, she seems alert to conversation around her. Propped on a dressed-up bed, she's a compatible roommate even for the young sophisticate who likes to camouflage her still-warm affection for dolls.

MATERIALS

½ yard red print fabric; red thread

¼ yard pink fabric; pink thread
scraps of blue, red and dark pink felt; thread to match
brown and pink embroidery floss
1 (⅜-inch) wooden dowel, 5 inches long
½ lb. polyester fiberfill
1¼ yards flat white lace, ⅜ inch wide
8½x9-inch piece of black vinyl fabric (very lightweight)
1 pair white baby socks, size newborn 3-4
¼ yard of white press-on interfacing
2 small white buttons for shoes
scrap of white fabric; white thread
40 yards white rug yarn
5½-inch strip of white seam binding
1 yard red satin ribbon
2 round white buttons for dress

DIRECTIONS

(Patterns are included on p.119; for directions on how to enlarge a pattern, see p. 97.)
1. Copy pattern pieces, enlarging as needed, and cut out. (All pattern pieces include a ¼-inch seam allowance, except for the tiny collar, which has a ⅛-inch allowance.)
2. Cut 2 body pieces, 4 arms, 2 cuffs and skirt from red print fabric folded right sides together. (Use arm pattern twice to make 4 pieces.)
3. Cut face from pink fabric. Cut 4 hands and 4 legs from pink fabric folded right sides together. (Use each pattern twice to make 4 pieces.)
4. Machine-stitch face to head section of one body piece, using zigzag stitch.

5. Cut eyes from blue felt, cheeks from pink felt and mouth from red felt. Hand-stitch to face. Embroider eyebrows, eyelashes and nose with brown and pink embroidery floss.

6. Place body pieces right sides together and machine-stitch around body and head from A to B, leaving bottom edge open. Trim neck seams to ⅛ inch.

7. Turn right side out and stuff head half full. Insert wooden dowel through neck to about eye level and continue stuffing. (Bottom of dowel will be in body.) Leave bottom edge of body open.

8. Machine-stitch hands to arm pieces, right sides together; make sure you have a front and back hand for each arm. Then pin front and back pieces of each arm right sides together and machine-stitch, leaving top edge open.

9. Turn arms and hands right side out and lightly stuff. Machine-stitch on top of hands and elbows as indicated by dotted lines on pattern.

10. Cut 2 pieces of lace, each 5¼ inches long. Turn bottom edge of each cuff under ⅛ inch and machine-stitch lace to this edge. Gather top edge of each cuff to fit arm. Turn gathered edges under and hand-stitch each cuff into position ¾ inch above wrist.

11. Cut 2 shoe tops (C) and 2 shoe bottoms (D) from black vinyl fabric.

12. Cut off cuffs of socks and set aside. From feet of socks, cut 2 squares, 1¾x1¾ inches. Reinforce squares of sock fabric with press-on interfacing.

13. Place shoe top (C) on top of one square; line up top edge of shoe with top edge of square. Machine-stitch, using zigzag stitch, around U-shaped open-

(continued on p. 119)

Calico Critters

These animal characters are sure to delight children—they're toys and treats all in one. Big Mouse and the three Little Critters begin as drawstring bags with some trimmings; the animals take shape when you fill the bags with candy or small gifts. When the original treat is gone, the bags can hold jacks, marbles or other small childhood treasures. Grownups enjoy them, too—they make perfect party favors or special gift wraps.

Little Critters

A single body pattern for these critters can be used to make a cat, bunny or mouse. Choose patterns for ears, paws and feet according to the critter you want to make; patterns are included on p. 122.

MATERIALS

scraps of fabric and matching thread
scraps of felt: black, red and two other colors
paper punch (optional)
white glue
a few inches of heavy white thread
small pompon (for bunny only)
16 inches of narrow ribbon

DIRECTIONS

1. Copy body pattern and cut two pieces from fabric.
2. Trace patterns on p. 122 for foot, paw, ear and inner ear of the critter of your choice; cut out.
3. Cut two inner ears from felt. From a second color of felt, cut two each of all other pattern pieces.
4. Punch or cut two black felt circles for eyes and a red felt circle for nose.
5. Place one body piece flat, right side up. On top, position ears (inner ear on top), paws and feet along the edges as shown on pattern, with pieces pointing toward center and straight edge of each piece extending slightly over the side of the fabric so that these pieces can be attached when seams are sewn.

6. Place second body piece on top, right side down. Machine-stitch sides and bottom, using ¼-inch seams; leave top open.
7. Turn body right side out. Paws, feet and ears should be in correct position. Add a dab of glue between inner and outer ears.
8. Glue eyes and nose to face.
9. To make whiskers, stitch two lengths of white thread under nose. (For bunny, glue small white pompon to back of body.)
10. To make casing for drawstring, turn top edge down ¼ inch, then turn again ½ inch. Stitch, leaving a small opening at back. Insert ribbon.

Big Mouse

MATERIALS

scraps of fabric and felt; thread to match
black felt-tipped pen
8½ inches of white cord, ¼ inch thick
small black pompon
white glue
heavy black thread
16 inches of white cord, ⅛ inch thick
6 inches of colored yarn (optional)

DIRECTIONS

1. Copy mouse pattern and cut out.
2. Cut two mouse ears from felt, using patterns on p. 122, and two body pieces from fabric.
3. Draw eyes on fabric with pen.
4. Place fabric pieces right sides together. To make tail, place 8½-inch-long cord between layers, with most of cord toward center. (One end of cord will be caught in seam.) Stitch fabric down front, across bottom and up back, leaving an inch open at top of back seam. Press seam allowances of this 1-inch opening to wrong side. Turn body right side out.
5. To make nose, sew black pompon to corner of fabric below eyes. To make whiskers, use 4 lengths of black thread, each 4 inches long; sew above nose and add a dab of glue to secure.
6. To make casing for drawstring, turn top edge down ¼ inch, then turn down again ½ inch. Position ears inside bag on top of casing. Straight edge will be caught in casing seam. Stitch casing. Insert white cord for drawstring.
7. Knot end of tail and trim tail with small yarn bow, if desired.

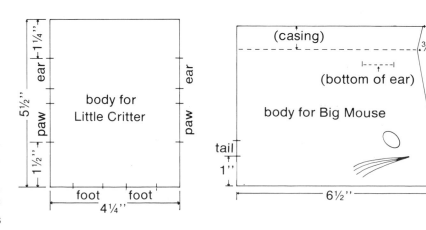

Childproof Decorations

One of the most beautiful forms of Christmas decoration is the Nativity, and a creche cut from pine is an appropriate way to honor Jesus, the son of a carpenter. Also shown is a Christmas tree made from a wooden dowel with natural pine ornaments to hang from its branches.

Unlike so many Christmas decorations that children are asked to admire—but told not to touch—these can be handled without danger of shattering or coming apart. Both the Nativity figures and the ornaments are free-standing, and their smooth surfaces are meant to be explored by little fingers. Fine sandpaper will eliminate any traces of fingerprint smudges.

Nativity

The base pictured is oak, stained walnut to contrast with the Nativity figures. Patterns are included on pp. 120-121.

TOOLS

jigsaw with fine blades
drill with $^1/_{16}$-inch, ⅛-inch and ⅜-inch bits

MATERIALS

1x7½x11½-inch piece of wood for base
fine sandpaper
walnut stain (optional)
carbon paper
1x8x16-inch piece of pine
1 (⅜-inch) dowel, 3 inches long
straw or greenery
1 (⅜-inch) dowel, 7½ inches long

DIRECTIONS

(For directions on how to enlarge patterns, see p. 97.)
1. Drill a ⅜-inch hole in rear center of base to hold dowel.
2. Sand base to clean and smooth. Stain walnut if desired.
3. Enlarge patterns for figures and use carbon paper to trace onto 1x8x16-inch pine.
4. Cut out with jigsaw, cutting slowly to avoid breaking blade.
5. Drill holes in figures as shown on patterns: $^1/_{16}$-inch holes for animal eyes; ⅛-inch hole for pig's tail; ⅜-inch holes at bottom of star and angel and at top of stable roof.
6. Sand figures to clean and smooth.
7. Arrange figures on base. Place 3-inch dowel in stable roof; place angel on top of dowel. Place 7½-inch dowel in hole in base; place star on top of dowel. Add straw or greenery.

Tree

Patterns for tree and ornaments are included on pp. 120-121.

TOOLS

jigsaw with fine blades
drill with ⅛-inch and ⅜-inch bits for wood
screwdriver

MATERIALS

1 (1-inch) dowel, 24 inches long
carbon paper
1x4x4½-inch piece of pine
fine sandpaper
1 (1½-inch) dowel screw
1x8x8-inch piece of pine for base
1 (1½-inch) wood screw
2 (⅜-inch) dowel rods, 8 inches long
2 (⅜-inch) dowel rods, 12 inches long
2 (⅜-inch) dowel rods, 16 inches long
red yarn (optional)

DIRECTIONS

1. Drill 3 sets of ⅜-inch holes through 24-inch dowel, spacing as in Fig. 1 (see p. 121). These will hold branches.
2. Drill a ⅛-inch hole in top and a ⅛-inch hole in bottom of trunk.
3. Using carbon paper, trace star pattern on 1x4x4½-inch piece of pine. Cut out with jigsaw. Sand to clean and smooth.
4. Drill a ⅛-inch hole in bottom of star. Fasten star to top of dowel tree trunk with 1½-inch dowel screw.
5. Find center of 1x8x8-inch

pine base by drawing an X from corner to corner. Drill a ⅛-inch hole through base. Countersink about ¼ inch on bottom of base.
6. Fasten tree trunk dowel to base with 1½-inch wood screw.
7. Insert 8-inch dowels in uppermost set of tree trunk holes; insert 12-inch dowels in middle of trunk; insert 16-inch dowels in bottom of trunk. (See Fig. 1.)
8. If desired, wrap trunk with yarn.

Ornaments

To make cutting of ornaments easier, use fine-grained white pine with no knots.

TOOLS

jigsaw with fine blades
drill with ⅛-inch bit for wood

MATERIALS

carbon paper
12 pieces 1x4x4½-inch pine
fine sandpaper
12 (10-inch) lengths of red yarn

DIRECTIONS

(For directions on how to enlarge a pattern, see p. 97.)
1. Enlarge patterns and use carbon paper to trace patterns onto pine. Trace each animal twice.
2. Cut out ornaments with jigsaw, cutting slowly to avoid breaking blade.
3. Drill ⅛-inch holes for eyes, pig's tail and holes for yarn as shown on patterns.
4. Sand ornaments to clean and smooth.
5. To hang ornaments, tie on yarn loops and arrange on tree.

Mouse House

A dollhouse doesn't have to be elaborate to shelter a miniature world all its own. The Mouse House, an A-frame dwelling custom-made for a family of toy field mice, has a sturdiness and a simplicity that give it a rustic charm.

Made from a single 9-foot pine board, the Mouse House has open sides which allow two children to play opposite one another with plenty of room for little hands to move about freely. Because of its durable construction, the house can withstand generations of energetic use, and it's easily moved from room to room or from floor to table.

Since every Mouse House needs at least one resident to make it a proper home, directions are included for making your own mice.

The Mouse House can accommodate a wide variety of casual furnishings, and decorating ideas also follow. You might want to add some home improvements later—wallpaper, a porch or even a sundeck. The possibilities are as endless as the desires of a young collector, and they're well within the reach of any young parents.

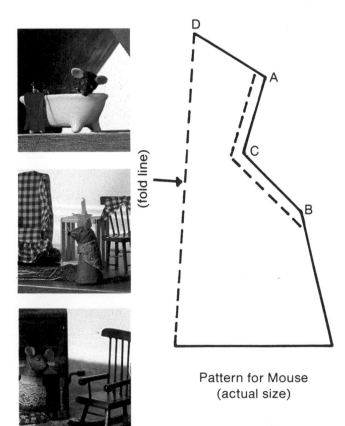

Pattern for Mouse
(actual size)

TOOLS

saw (power or hand)
hammer
nail set
protractor
T-square or artist's triangle (for making accurate right angles)

MATERIALS

1x12-inch pine board, 9 feet long
white glue
sixpenny finishing nails
plastic wood
sandpaper
stain

DIRECTIONS

1. Mark pine board into lengths for floors, walls and roof. (See diagram.) Cut roof.
2. Bevel top ends of roof (16 inches) with 38-degree bevels. Glue and nail beveled ends together to form a 76-degree angle. Keep boards flush at edges. Wipe off excess glue as you go.
3. Cut first-floor board (15 inches). Cut walls.
4. Bevel top ends of walls (13¾ inches) with 38-degree bevels. Glue and nail square ends of walls at right angle to bottom floorboard.
5. Position roof on sides of house so peak is centered. Glue and nail roof to walls.
6. Cut second-floor board (15 inches). Glue and nail in position 7 inches above the bottom floorboard. Cut attic floorboard.
7. Bevel attic floorboard (12½ inches) with 52-degree bevels on both ends. Position in angle of roof 7 inches below peak so it is level. Glue and nail.
8. Countersink all nails and fill with plastic wood.
9. Sand surfaces and edges smooth and apply stain.

How to Make a Mouse

Every Mouse House needs a mouse or more to make it a home. Here's how to make as many as you please. Dressing them is up to you.

MATERIALS

felt: gray, brown or gold for mouse body; pink for ears; thread to match
cotton
pink crewel yarn
brush with 1-inch bristles
white glue
blue and black thread

DIRECTIONS

(For directions on how to make a satin stitch, see p. 99.)
1. Trace pattern, transfer to felt folded right sides together and cut out. Be sure to place fold line on fold of fabric. Cut along solid lines.
2. Open felt and place flat. Bring together A and B and machine-stitch a dart, sewing along dotted line from A/B to C. Repeat on opposite side.
3. Fold along fold line, right sides together. Machine-stitch along raw edge from point of nose (D) to bottom edge, using ⅛-inch seam allowance. Leave bottom edge open. Turn inside out and stuff with cotton.
4. To make a 2-inch tail, knot together 3 strands of crewel *(continued on next page)*

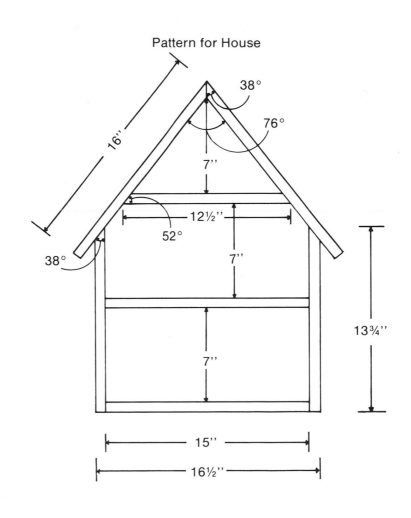

Pattern for House

yarn, secure knot with pin, and braid yarn. Knot bottom when braided.

5. Cut a 1-inch circle from felt (same color as body) for base of mouse. Place circle on bottom of mouse and whipstitch around edge, stitching tail in position at center back as you go.

6. To make whiskers, cut 3 bristles from brush, about ¾ inch long. Place bristles flat, crossing each other at the center. Dot center with white glue and allow to dry.

7. Hand-stitch whiskers to nose with black thread, stitching up and down around center. Sew between whiskers to keep them separated. Finish with a satin stitch to form nose.

8. Cut two ½-inch circles from pink felt. Cut a pie-shaped wedge from each. Pull cut edges of circles together and sew, forming small cupped ears. Sew ears to head where the cut edges are secured.

9. Satin-stitch small round eyes, using blue thread.

Furnishing a Mouse House

Basic Mouse House furniture can be constructed from common household items and fabric scraps and supplemented with standard dollhouse furniture.

Beds: Use rectangular gift boxes such as those made for jewelry or wallets. Cover with fabric to make single or double beds. Place open side down and secure fabric edges to inside of box. Headboard and footboard can be made from a row of Popsicle sticks cut to desired lengths and glued to the ends of the bed for support.

A more elaborate headboard can be made by soaking string in white glue. Squeeze off excess glue; place string on waxed paper in circular patterns, the same width as bed. Allow design to harden. Pinch off paper, leaving string design intact. Glue to head of bed, using Popsicle sticks for legs.

Chest of Drawers: Glue three small matchboxes on top of each other so that trays slide out as drawers. Cover with bright self-adhesive paper or fabric. Glue beads on drawer fronts as knobs.

Cradle: Use a small, oblong anchovy can with lid removed. File down sharp edges and line can with heavy quilted fabric to cover edges. Glue two semi-circular pieces of cardboard to bottom of can for rockers.

Or, cut a paper towel tube in half lengthwise. Then cut about 3 inches from half of tube. Cut a circle of cardboard slightly larger than height of tube. Cut circle in half and glue halves, straight side up, to both ends of cut tube. Cover or paint.

Decorative Bowls: Fill half a walnut shell with tiny balls of yarn rolled from embroidery thread.

Fireplace: Cut a rectangle from one end of a square box lid. Opening should be centered between sides of lid. Stand cut lid against wall. Cut a slightly longer and wider piece of cardboard for mantel and glue to box. (A paint stirrer covered with fabric also could be used for mantel.) For logs, cut cinnamon sticks, put a few inside box opening and stack the rest nearby.

Flower Accents: Arrange tiny strawflowers in small glass perfume bottles or in lids from food coloring bottles and secure with glue or clay.

Footstool: Cut a half-inch ring from the end of a paper towel tube. Cover with fabric, bending rough edges to the inside. Place the ring flat and cut a circular piece of cardboard slightly larger than the ring. Pad on side with cotton and cover with fabric, wrapping fabric edges to center of flat side. Glue flat side to ring base.

Lamp: Use the cap from a tube of toothpaste or a bottle of nail polish remover. Cut the narrow end of a golf tee to the desired height and glue into cap. (Wide end of tee becomes base.) Other lamp bases can be made from corks, play dough or large wooden beads. Be sure to flatten bottom surfaces.

Mirrors: Remove small cosmetic mirror from plastic container and glue onto thin cardboard cut slightly larger. Glue string or yarn around the cut edge of mirror, leaving a loop for hanging.

Picnic Bench: Line up 3 or 4 Popsicle sticks and glue 2 supporting sticks across them. Cut to desired size. For legs, use 2 sticks crossed to form an X at each end of bench. Cut sticks at angles to fit against top of bench.

Picnic Table: Make same way as bench, with longer legs.

Picture Frames: Use white lids from prescription bottles and glue circular photos or pictures inside. Hang these on the wall along with tiny keys and coins for an interesting wall grouping.

Round Table: Line up 4 or 5 Popsicle sticks and glue 2 supporting sticks flat across them. Cut in circle (using an X-acto blade, if you have one). Glue on thread spool as pedestal base.

Toy Chest: Glue Popsicle sticks to all sides of a small cardboard box and paint or stain.

Enjoying Christmas with Your Children

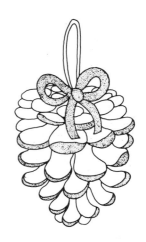

By CHANNELS TO CHILDREN

Give your preschool children a special gift this holiday season—you.

If you take time to work together on a few simple yuletide activities, you'll find communication increasing and a special closeness developing. Your children will have an opportunity to express feelings, develop creativity and establish traditions that they can someday share with their own children. You'll find that when time and talents are shared, Christmas takes on a new meaning of family togetherness that will be treasured long after toys have been broken or forgotten.

Choose the projects that best suit your child's needs and abilities. Before you begin, collect all the necessary materials and talk about what you will be doing or making. Provide a relaxed atmosphere with ample space and time to complete the activity.

Most of all, be realistic in your expectations of what your child can do, and remember that the process is more important than the end result. Lend support, show interest and be generous in your praise.

TRIMMING THE TREE

The Christmas tree offers a unique display area for art work. Any of these simple ornaments will add a personal touch to your tree as well as a twinkle to the eyes of the proud artist.

● **Pine Cone Ornament:** Place a little white tempera in a shallow container. Roll a pine cone in paint to cover tips of the cone and allow to dry. To hang, wrap one end of a pipe cleaner around the cone and make a hook with the other end.

● **Aluminum Ornaments:** Draw designs on aluminum foil and cut out. (Use aluminum foil cake pans, pie plates, or frozen food containers.) For example, cut a strip of aluminum and curl it into a spiral by wrapping it around a pencil; or draw a circle or free-form shape, cut the edges to form a fringe, and bend alternate fringed sections in opposite directions. For a hanger, open a paper clip into an S shape and hook to ornament.

● **Rigatoni Wreath:** Dye rigatoni by dipping in water mixed with food coloring, or spray with silver or gold paint. Allow to dry on waxed paper. String 5 or 6 rigatoni on ribbon. Tie strands together and curl ends of ribbon by pulling over blade of scissors.

● **Memory Ornaments:** Decorating the tree can be a time to reflect upon the past year. Talk over significant events that happened to each family member and the family as a whole. Choose one event for each person or the family and create an ornament to symbolize that event, labeling the ornament with the year it represents. Save ornaments to display each year, and trimming the Christmas tree will become a time to reminisce about the important events of previous years.

For example, glue a photo taken during the family vacation onto a small map of the area you visited or onto a brochure from a tourist attraction. Spray with clear varnish. You also could make a photo ornament for each family member or for a new addition to the family. Punch a hole in the top edge of the lid from a baby food jar and glue a photo to the inside of the lid. Spread rubber cement on the outer top and sides of lid, sprinkle with glitter and allow to dry. Thread string through the hole and tie to form a loop.

GIFTS TO MAKE

Explain to your child that many things can be given as gifts—that presents don't have to be purchased but can be made, and that doing things for others is also an act of giving.

(continued on next page)

Offer examples of helping others. Explain that the reason for giving is to show family and friends love and affection, and emphasize that the most important aspect of giving is the thought.
Here are three gifts your child can make:
- **Dried-Flower Terrarium:** Place a small amount of clay or play dough in baby food jar. (To make play dough, mix to desired consistency 2 tsp. flour, 1 tsp. salt and about 1 tsp. water.) Arrange dried flowers and weeds about an inch high in the clay. Place jar over dried arrangement and secure lid. Glue red ribbon around the edge of the lid.
- **"Batik Handkerchief":** Have your child draw a picture with crayons on a white handkerchief. Cover hankie with paper. To set crayon design, your child will need your help: press handkerchief with warm iron.
- **"Stained Glass" Candle Holder:** Cover a baby food jar with various pieces of colored tissue paper that have been dipped in liquid starch. Allow to dry and place a small candle inside jar.

EXPRESSING EMOTIONS

Emotions may surge during this season. Help your child deal with these strong feelings by encouraging their expression. Explain that happiness and excitement may be accompanied by unexplained sadness, impatience, and possibly jealousy. Rivalry among siblings and friends is understandable when presents and toys are so plentiful. Sadness may be felt if a loved one is away and cannot share in the season's festivities.

Since Christmas excitement begins many weeks before the actual holiday, the wait often seems endless to a child. These activities can help:
- **Christmas Symbols:** Each day, discuss a Christmas symbol and its meaning. Symbols can be purchased ornaments or pictures cut from magazines or greeting cards. Each symbol can be hung on the Christmas tree or taped to a calendar.

Each major symbol can be explained simply. For example: *Joseph* is the husband of Mary; *Mary* is the mother of Jesus; the *manger* is the place where Mary laid Jesus; an *angel* came to the shepherds telling them of the birth of Jesus; *Three Wise Men* bearing treasures came to see Jesus; a *star* represents the Star of Bethlehem, which guided the Wise Men to Baby Jesus; *candles* symbolize the light that Jesus brought to earth; *Christmas tree lights* represent Christ as the "Light of the World," and also represent stars; *bells* rang to announce the coming of Jesus; an *evergreen tree* was decorated by pagan people at a winter feast as a sign that winter would end and warmth would return; *Saint Nicholas* was a generous bishop who brought presents to children and needy people.
- **Calendar Chain:** A week before Christmas, make a calendar chain and bell. Cut 1-inch-wide strips of red and green construction paper; make a circle from one strip by gluing ends together. Place another strip through the circle, overlapping ends and gluing. Repeat, making a loop for each day until Christmas. Attach a paper bell to the chain and write this verse on the bell:

It seems the Christmas season
Is the longest time of year.
How many days before Old Santa will appear?
Take a link from this bell
When the Sandman is at the door—
Christmas Eve will be here
When there are no more!

Each evening, recite the verse and remove one loop from the chain to help your child determine how many days until Christmas.

When an adult shares time, feelings and attitudes with a young person, Christmas develops a special meaning. Not only do traditions begin, but memories of childhood Christmases will remain for years to come.

How to Become a Gift Detective

Clues to the perfect gift are everywhere—once you learn to spot them

Finding just the right gifts for people you love—one of the greatest joys of Christmas—can become one of the season's greatest frustrations, especially when the search is carried out amid mobs of shoppers.

Many country women solve the gift dilemma each year, delighting friends and families with their choices, without going near a department store. How? By thinking about the people they want to please.

Like professional sleuths, they search for clues. It's easy to give the perfect gift to every person on your list once you know what each one is interested in and enjoys.

Listen when your husband complains that his favorite hunting knife is wearing out. React when your niece exclaims, "Oh, what a great book on raising dogs." Start looking for material when your grandson admires the flannel shirt you made for his grandfather.

It's helpful to have a little notebook in which to jot down the hints that friends and family inadvertently drop throughout the year. Then you can sleuth all year long as you browse through catalogs and poke through garage sales, antique shops, specialty stores and museum shops.

Set aside a corner of a closet or shelf to store all your do-ahead shopping—labeled, of course. (Otherwise, when it comes time in December to wrap Aunt Dolly's gift, you might forget what you bought her in February, or where you put it.)

Even if you wait till December to start your search, you don't have to give up the idea of an individual present. Just search your memory for clues.

(continued on next page)

A Kentucky woman recalled that her son-in-law had enjoyed riding a borrowed bicycle to work all summer long. On Christmas day he found a shiny new ten-speed bike under the tree, a present from his in-laws, and he was as thrilled as a child.

The most personal gift of all may be one that costs nothing, especially if you're lucky enough to be able to give a remembrance from the past.

A farm wife from Indiana refinished and restored a treasured springboard wagon seat that had belonged to her husband's dad. "My husband told me he had never received a present that surprised and touched him so much," she said.

A great-aunt gave a Kansas couple their favorite gift: her marriage certificate, dated 1902, which she had had framed.

A Nebraska woman received a family heirloom she had always admired, a kerosene lamp that had been a wedding gift to her husband's great-grandparents in 1879.

A thoughtful Michigan farmer knew his grown daughter would appreciate a touch of home, so he saved wood from a tree that had to be removed from the family farm and turned it into a beautiful magazine rack, which he presented to his daughter for use in her own home.

Each time two little girls from Louisiana visited their grandmother, they admired her pine needle sewing baskets, which had been in the family for a century. For Christmas, Grandma gave each girl a basket. Another grandmother retrieved a steel doll trunk and cradle from the attic for her granddaughter.

Even if you don't have something old to pass along, the sentimental gift might be right there, just waiting for your discerning eye to spot it.

A Little Leaguer in Kentucky was the happiest kid in town when his Dad transformed his baseball bat into a trophy. The bat, which the boy had used

to hit his first home run, had been engraved with his name and the date of the grand occasion.

A Mississippi mother gathered photos, newspaper clippings and other mementos from her son's school days, from kindergarten through high school, into a scrapbook. It was his Christmas present his senior year, and he loved it.

A North Dakota couple was given a large photo of the International Peace Gardens, where they first met. A Vermont farmer gave his wife a photo taken years before of the family farm.

And an Alabama woman, still silently grieving for a favorite Siamese cat which had died months earlier, was touched to find that her husband understood—his gift to her was a Siamese kitten with identical markings.

Perhaps your clue is a hobby.

"My brother was aware that my son collected guns," said a South Dakota farm mother, "so he searched through flea markets and found an old gun catalog dated 1918-1919. My son said it was his favorite gift."

An aunt knew her nephew loved old coins, so she stopped by a coin store and bought him Indian-head pennies he couldn't afford to add to his collection. A hog farmer spied a little planter shaped like a pig and knew he had the perfect gift to add to his wife's growing collection of novelty pigs.

A special interest can inspire many gift ideas. An Indiana couple whose daughter is an expert horsewoman attended every horse show and watched with pride as she and her steed jumped the fences. They also photographed each event. Then they selected the very best of the photos, had them enlarged and framed, and gave them to her for Christmas.

A food fancy can point the way to a different kind of gift. A ten-year-old boy gave his big brother, who is a pickle freak, a gallon of dill pickles tied with a big red bow.

If your family seems intrigued with its past, take a hint from an Iowa woman who carefully traced the family tree and compiled a geneology that was a welcome gift for every family member on her list.

Sometimes a practical gift is the best gift—because it shows you recognize a real need. An Illinois husband who had watched his wife trying to cope with returning to college and keeping house at the same time gave her an I.O.U. for a weekly visit by a housekeeper.

These gift-givers have discovered how to make the holidays more rewarding, and so can you—once you learn to be alert to the clues that will take the mystery out of your Christmas shopping.

Appendix

HOW TO ENLARGE A PATTERN

Many patterns in this book are shown on grids and must be enlarged. In most cases, each square on a grid represents a 1-inch square on a full-sized pattern.

To enlarge a pattern, count the number of vertical and horizontal lines shown on the grid of the pattern you wish to copy. Then on graph paper, tracing paper, brown wrapping paper or other paper, draw an equal number of lines spaced 1 inch apart; this will produce a grid of 1-inch squares.

Next, copy the pattern from the small squares to the corresponding large squares, working square by square until you have enlarged the complete design. On large or complex patterns, you may wish to number the lines across the top and down one side (on both the small grid and the enlargement) to make it easier to keep track of your work.

HOW TO TRANSFER PATTERN DETAILS TO FABRIC, WOOD AND CARDBOARD

There are several ways to transfer pattern details such as lines to be embroidered, sections to be cut apart or holes to be punched or drilled. Choose the method that you think will work best for the materials you are using. When working with fabric, test the method you plan to use on a scrap of the material.

To transfer to fabric: Trace patterns on tracing paper. Turn paper over and blacken lines on back with a soft lead pencil or a transfer pencil. Position tracing paper on right side of fabric with transfer lines down. If you use a soft pencil, rub the design with your finger or with the rounded edge of a pen. If you use a transfer pencil, press the paper with a warm iron.

Another way to mark fabric is to place dressmaker's carbon between pattern and fabric. Retrace pattern with a soft pencil, being careful not to smudge other areas.

A third way is to place pattern on fabric and, with a sharp pencil, punch holes through paper to make dots along pattern lines. Use a sharp white or yellow drawing pencil for dark-colored fabrics.

To transfer to wood or cardboard: Trace pattern on tracing paper. Blacken pattern lines with soft pencil on back of tracing paper, as for fabric. Then place paper on wood or cardboard, transfer lines down, and retrace lines with a sharp pencil.

A second method is to use carbon paper between pattern and wood or cardboard. Trace pattern details with a soft pencil, being careful not to smudge other areas.

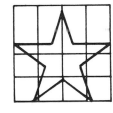

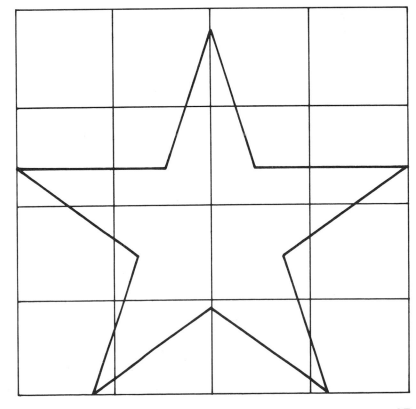

Appendix

HOW TO MAKE EMBROIDERY STITCHES

Anchored Loop: Bring needle and thread up through fabric. Take a tiny stitch, splitting thread as needle comes up again. Leave a loop, and take another tiny stitch across the bottom to anchor it.

Backstitch: Work from right to left. Bring needle and thread up through fabric. Insert needle a little to the right and bring needle up an equal distance ahead. For next stitch, go back so you can insert needle at beginning of last stitch; this eliminates spaces between the stitches.

Blanket Stitch: Work from left to right. Bring needle and thread from behind fabric (at lower edge of design or at cut edge of fabric). Hold a loop of thread down with your left thumb. Take a vertical stitch, bringing needle over loop. Leave a small space between stitches; this will vary with the thickness of the yarn or thread you are using.

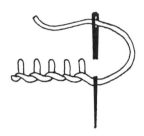

Buttonhole Stitch: Work the same as for the blanket stitch, but make the stitches closer together.

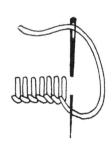

Chain Stitch: Bring needle and thread up through fabric. Make a loop with thread and hold it in place with your left thumb. Insert needle into fabric where thread last came up, then take a short stitch ahead, drawing needle over loop.

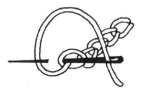

Couching Stitch: One thread will lie on top of the fabric and form a design line. Fasten the end of this thread on the wrong side of the fabric with a knot or with small stitches. Then bring the thread to the right side and pin it into position. To fasten this thread, work with a needle and another thread. Make tiny, evenly spaced stitches, catching the design thread to the fabric.

French Knot: Bring needle and thread up through fabric. Keep thread taut and wrap it one to three times around tip of needle. (The more loops you make, the larger the knot.) Insert needle very close to the place where thread came up, and slowly pull thread to the back of fabric.

Long and Short Stitches: Make a row of stitches, alternating long and short straight stitches, following outline of design. Then fill in design with long stitches, keeping them close together as in the satin stitch.

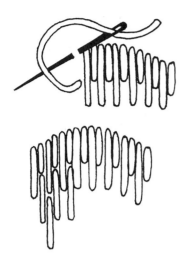

Running Stitch: Work from right to left, keeping stitches the same size and evenly spaced.

Satin Stitch: Bring needle and thread up at one edge of design and insert it at opposite edge. Take needle and thread under design and bring needle up again next to the first stitch. Keep stitches close together so that fabric does not show through.

Split Stitch: Work from left to right. Begin with a small straight stitch, taking needle and thread to back of fabric. Bring needle up so that it splits thread at center of last stitch.

Stem Stitch: Work from left to right. Make a small stitch, slanting it slightly across line of work. Keep thread below needle as you work.

The Christmas Story

(continued from p. 5)

This crewel embroidery is 5½ x 14½ inches and is done in fine wool yarn on linen, with embroidery floss for flesh tones. Use single strands of wool (separated from 3-ply crewel yarn) and single strands of embroidery floss. The numbers on the pattern indicate colors. Work with fabric held in an embroidery hoop. The finished piece can be framed or mounted on a thin base of heavy cardboard or wood.

MATERIALS

linen, cream-colored, 10x20 inches
tracing paper, 10x20 inches
transfer pencil
embroidery hoop
crewel embroidery needle
embroidery floss, flesh-colored
Persian-type crewel yarn

This pattern uses 14 colors of crewel yarn. Choose your own colors or use those shown. To copy exactly, you will need 2 small skeins each of light blue, medium blue and royal blue, and 1 small skein each of gray, brown, green, yellow, rust, orange, purple, violet, black, gold and white.

DIRECTIONS

1. On tracing paper, trace pattern. Add all color numbers, and *(continued on next page)*

make a chart pairing numbers with colors you've chosen to use.

2. Transfer pattern to linen. Be sure to center pattern, leaving a margin on all sides.

3. Embroider the design as follows: Let stitches follow design lines, such as the flow of the robes and sleeves and the body contour of the donkey. Begin with the river, working (1), then (2), then (3), using a split stitch. Follow horizontal lines first, then fan out with the curves.

4. Work inn (4) with vertical satin stitch. Add door and windows (14) in vertical satin stitch. Work

dome (9) in stem stitch, following curve. Add one straight stitch at top of dome.

5. Work tree trunk (5) and palm leaves (6) in stem stitch.

6. Work Mary's veil and sleeve (3) in split stitch. Work her cape (2) in split stitch. Use stem stitch across the bottom of veil (3).

7. Work Joseph's collar and undersleeve (10) in split stitch. Use split stitch for robe (11), then add stem stitch to outline the sleeve of his robe (10).

8. Work donkey (8) with split stitch. Use satin stitch inside donkey ears (9) and a straight stitch for his nose (9). For his

mane (9), make anchored loops to fill area, using loops about ½ inch long. When finished, clip loops, brush yarn, then clip to about ¼ inch.

9. Use chain stitch for Joseph's hair (5). Work one circle at a time.

10. Use chain stitch for Mary's hair (13).

11. With embroidery floss (15), use a split stitch for faces, hands and feet.

12. Use satin stitch for eyes (12) of Mary, Joseph and donkey.

13. Use long and short stitch to fill halos (7).

14. Work cane (5) with satin

stitches going across cane. Use straight stitch for soles and straps of Joseph's sandals (5).

15. Work donkey's hooves (4) with satin stitch.

16. Press finished work, using a clean cloth to protect surface.

17. Frame or mount on a firm base, wrapping border fabric over edges and securing on the back.

COLOR CODE

1. light blue	9. orange
2. medium blue	10. purple
3. royal blue	11. violet
4. gray	12. black
5. brown	13. gold
6. green	14. white
7. yellow	15. flesh (floss)
8. rust	

A Mug of Good Wishes

(continued from p. 53)

MATERIALS

pewter mug
Oasis (or other
  floral foam)
small pine cones (about 12)
beading wire (or other fine wire)
white glue
wreath
cotton ribbon: 1 or 2 colors in
  plaid or calico prints

DIRECTIONS

1. Place a piece of Oasis in bottom of mug.
2. Wrap a piece of wire around large end of one pine cone.
3. Dip other end of wire into white glue. Insert glue-covered end into Oasis base in mug.
4. Repeat with each pine cone until mouth of mug is filled.
5. Wrap a length of wire around mug and mug handle and attach mug to wreath frame.
6. Make an assortment of small ribbon bows. Space evenly around wreath; attach with wire.

Yuletide Tub

MATERIALS

large galvanized washtub
sand
newspaper
large pine cones to fill tub
greenery
red gingham ribbon, 2¾
  inches wide
masking tape

DIRECTIONS

1. Fill bottom of tub with sand to keep tub stable.
2. Fill tub halfway with wadded-up newspaper.
3. Arrange pine cones and sprigs of greenery in tub.
4. Wrap ribbon around tub and add a large bow.
5. Secure the ribbon to the tub with tape.

A Christmas Carol

MATERIALS

holiday sheet music
12x16-inch sheet of plywood or
  particle board, ½ inch thick
  (or ready-made decorative
  plaque)
paintbrush
wood stain
white glue
decoupage transfer emulsion
hook for hanging

DIRECTIONS

1. If sheet music is new, singe edges over candle flame.
2. Brush stain on backing board and let dry.
3. Glue sheet music to board, centering it so that margin is even on all sides.
4. Apply decoupage transfer emulsion, following manufacturer's directions.
5. Attach hook to back of board at top center.

Skater's Wreath

MATERIALS

1 pair child's white ice skates
pressure-sensitive vinyl plastic
  letters, red
large green wreath
red gingham cotton ribbon,
  ¾ inches wide
beading wire

DIRECTIONS

1. Clean and polish skates.
2. Press letters onto skates, spacing evenly and using photo as a guide.
3. Attach skates to wreath frame, using wire to fasten securely.
4. Make small puffy bows from gingham ribbon and attach to skates with wire.

Blackboard

MATERIALS

blackboard with wooden frame
hook for hanging
sandpaper
red enamel
paintbrush
heavy staples; hammer
small pine boughs
holly
white chalk

DIRECTIONS

1. If blackboard has no hook for hanging, attach hook to back of wooden frame at top center.
2. Lightly sand wooden frame.
3. Paint frame with red enamel. Let dry.
4. Using staples and hammer, attach pine boughs and sprigs of holly to top center of frame.
5. Use white chalk to write your holiday message in letters as bold as possible so that they will be easy to read.

Toy Soldier Banner

(continued from p. 55)

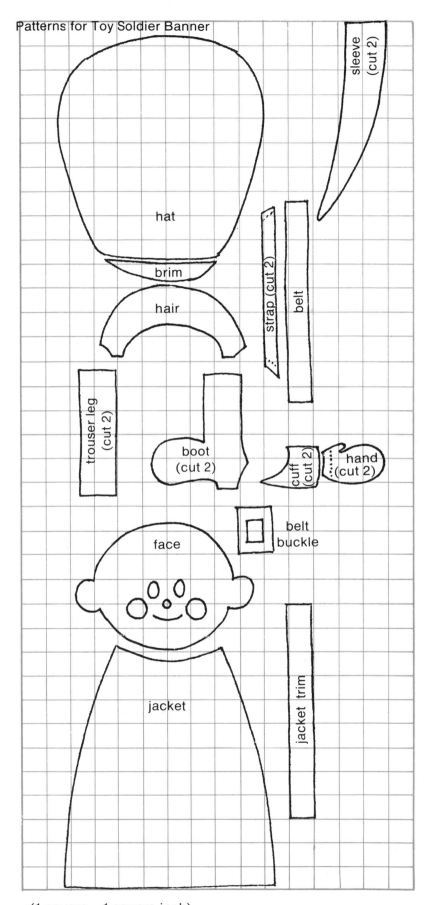

Patterns for Toy Soldier Banner

sleeve (cut 2)

hat

brim

strap (cut 2)

belt

hair

trouser leg (cut 2)

boot (cut 2)

cuff (cut 2)

hand ((cut 2)

belt buckle

face

jacket

jacket trim

(1 square = 1 square inch)

Love Banner

(continued from p. 55)

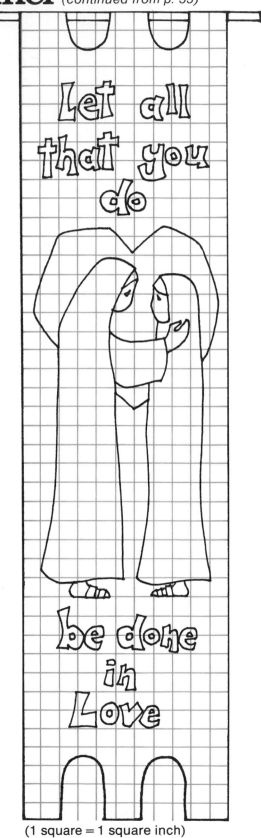

Let all that you do

be done in Love

(1 square = 1 square inch)

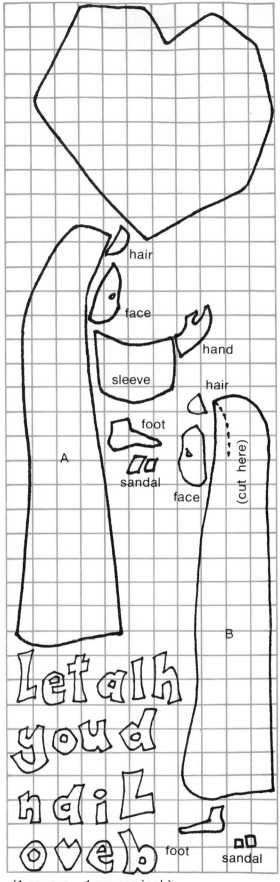

hair

face

hand

sleeve

hair

A

foot

sandal

face

(cut here)

B

Let alh youd ndiL oveb

foot

sandal

(1 square = 1 square inch)

Three Kings Banner

(continued from p. 56)

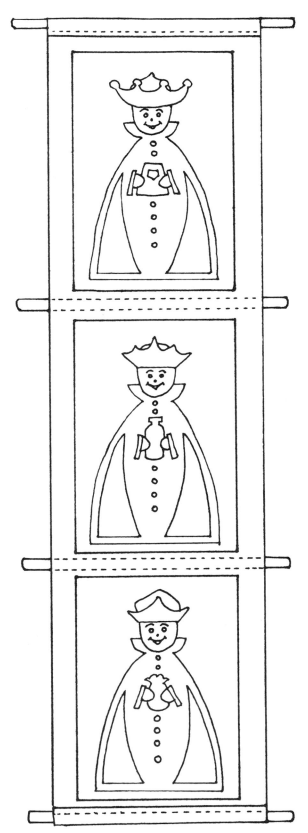

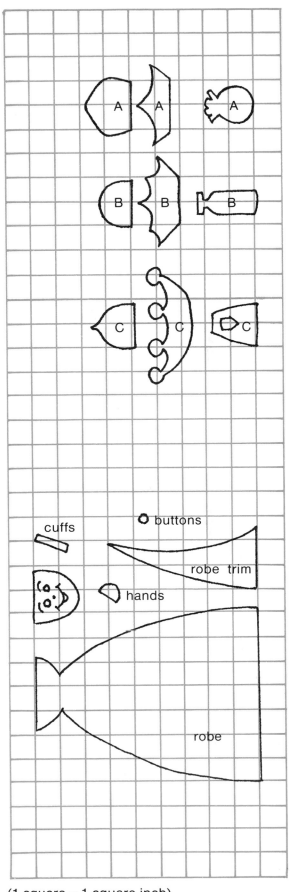

cuffs

buttons

robe trim

hands

robe

(1 square = 1 square inch)

Big Splash (continued from p. 61)

106   (1 square = 1 square inch)

(1 square = 1 square inch)

Patchwork

(continued from p. 66)

stitch as in Step 7. Repeat three times to make four finished petals.

9. Fold ring strip in half lengthwise, right sides together, and stitch across top and down the side, using a ¼-inch seam allowance. Turn to right side.

10. Form a ring and whip the ends together with handstitches.

11. Assemble poinsettia on ring (see Fig. 1). Place the two green leaves on top of ring, hiding ring seam and overlapping leaves about 1¼ inches. Hand-stitch in place.

12. Place two red petals on top, at right angles to leaves, with petals overlapping about ¾ inch. Stitch in place.

13. Place remaining two petals on top, overlapping and at right angles to the first set of petals. Edges of leaves should show below petals. Stitch in place.

14. Make cording for center. Fold cording strip lengthwise so that raw edges meet at center (right side out), and press. Fold strip in half lengthwise, with raw edges inside. Stitch down center of strip.

15. Fasten one end of cording strip to center of petal. Make about five folds in strip, tacking each fold to center of petal, and hiding raw ends under folds.

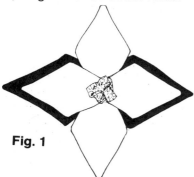

Fig. 1

Cornhusk

(continued from p. 69)

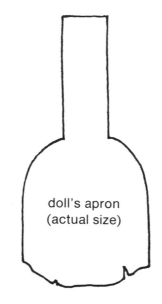

doll's apron
(actual size)

10. Trace pattern for doll apron and cut from husk.

11. Apron and skirt are tied on upside down, with bottom of skirt over doll's head. Place apron over face, with narrow extension below waist. Push arms up alongside head (Fig. 8).

Fig. 8

12. For full skirt, use 10 or 12 large husks. If husk has triangular shape, keep pointed end down, and place husk a little below waist. Add additional husks, overlapping as you work. Tie tightly at waist (Fig. 9). Cut

Fig. 9

across ragged edge at bottom of doll; this leaves about 2 inches for body. Now, peel down skirt like a banana so that skirt is in correct position; apron will be on top of skirt. Cut across bottom of skirt to make even. Use bobby pins or hair clips to hold bottom of skirt together. Place skirt over glass to dry. When dry, glue top layers of skirt together.

13. For hair, you can use wet or dry corn silk. Place silk flat and tie with brown thread at middle to form a part. Put glue on doll's head; arrange corn silk on head with part at the top. Tie a pony tail behind neck (Fig. 10), then

Fig. 10

bring tail up to form a bun on the back of the head. Tuck ends of silk and string inside bun at top, and glue. If braids are desired, take three lengths of silk, and braid them together. (If you use wet silk, let it dry.) Glue braid around bun. **Note:** If bonnet is used, hair should be left straight—no bun. To make hair curl below bonnet, roll wet silk up in back, and fasten at neck with a bobby pin. Let dry.

14. To make bonnet, cut a 2x 2½-inch piece of husk. Make two ¼-inch folds along one edge of wide side. Place the wet bonnet on top of doll's head and hair, with folded edge outside and at front. Form bonnet by pinning to head. Let dry to shape of head; glue in place.

15. For bows at front and back of apron, take a ¼-inch strip of husk and tie into a bow. Let dry and glue in place. Use a ⅛-inch strip to make bow for back of hair or bonnet.

Flower

The petals for the husk flowers shown are glued to a dried flower center, which was purchased.

MATERIALS

cornhusks
dried flower center, such as daisy head (available at craft stores or florists)
florist's tape
white glue that dries clear
thin wire

DIRECTIONS

1. Use pattern for petal to cut about six petals from husks. (Flowers can be made any size by varying size of petals.)
2. Bend petals with a pencil, curling wide edge of petal around pencil.
3. Dip pointed end of petal in glue and place in the dried flower head (Fig. 1). Add more petals, circling the flower head and overlapping petals as you work.
4. To make stem, push the end of an 8-inch length of thin wire up into the bottom of flower head. Wrap wire with florist's tape.

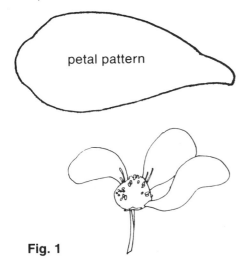

petal pattern

Fig. 1

Star

Work with dry husks for this design. The finished star will be about 4 inches across.

MATERIALS

cardboard (for circle base)
cornhusks
white glue
thin wire
wooden bead
gold cord

DIRECTIONS

1. From cardboard, make a 2-inch circle.
2. From dry husk, cut a ¾x4-inch strip. Moisten just enough to bend the strip and cross ends, forming a point (Fig. 1). Cut off ends beyond point (dotted lines in Fig. 1), and glue together. Repeat six times, to make a total of seven points.
3. Cut seven small flat star points, ½x¾ inches (see pattern).
4. With wire, make a loop ¾ inch long; leave 1-inch ends beyond loop.
5. Cover cardboard with glue. Place wire on circle, with loop extending beyond circle. Next, cover this same side (and wire ends) with a piece of husk. When dry, trim husk to edge of circle. This is the back of the star.
6. Smear glue over front of circle. Keep wire loop at top. Arrange the seven curled points to form a star. Glue the seven flat points behind and between the curved points (Fig. 2). Let dry.
7. Glue wooden bead to center of star. Glue gold cord around edge of circle to finish back.

Clothespin

(continued from p. 71)

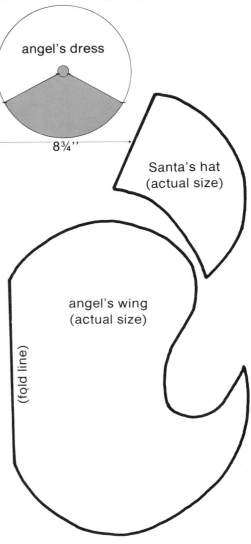

angel's dress

8¾''

Santa's hat
(actual size)

angel's wing
(actual size)

(fold line)

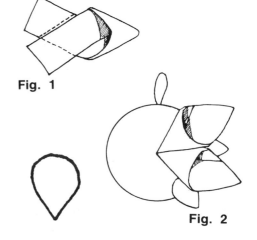

Fig. 1

Fig. 2

(continued from p. 72)
SUPPLIES

Paper for cards may be purchased at an art supply store or anyplace where good-quality papers, colored on both sides, are sold. The papers used for our cards are 80-lb. text (medium weight) with a vellum (smooth) finish.

TIPS FOR USING RUBBER CEMENT

1. Apply glue to each surface and let dry.
2. Use tracing paper between dry surfaces while positioning papers exactly. When positioned, carefully tear a corner or piece of tracing paper from between glued surfaces to let a small area of the glued surfaces meet. This will tack them in place.
3. Repeat, if necessary, in other places until papers are secure enough not to slip. Then remove all the tracing paper and press surfaces together.
4. Remove any excess rubber cement with a rubber cement ''pick-up,'' or by rubbing gently with your fingertip.

MATERIALS

colored papers
can of rubber cement with brush
rubber cement ''pick-up'' (optional)
metal ruler (to use in cutting and folding)
X-acto knife
sharp scissors
tracing paper
compass (helpful for drawing curves for Santa and Crown designs)
paper punch (for Santa and Tree)
pinking shears (for House and

Santa)
legal seals (available at stationery stores)

See directions for individual cards to help you determine how much paper you need.

House

MATERIALS

yellow paper, 6x8½ inches
orange paper, 5x9 inches
dark green paper: 6x9 inches
   plus 8x12 inches for envelope
light green paper, 1½x1½
   inches square

DIRECTIONS

(For directions on how to enlarge a pattern, see p. 97.)
1. Copy patterns, enlarging as needed.
2. Using pattern as a guide, cut out front of house from yellow paper. Cut on solid lines and fold on dotted lines. Carefully fold open shutters, and partially fold open door. Fold sides in accordian fold, as shown in Fig. 1.
3. Cut out three candles, using pattern. Glue to inside of each window, lining up dotted line with bottom edge of window.
4. Cut out liner from orange paper, using pattern, and slip between surfaces A and B. Place house face down as in Fig. 2.
5. Holding liner in place, fold out A flaps and glue inside of A flaps. Glue corresponding area

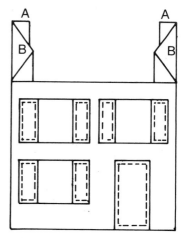

Fig. 1

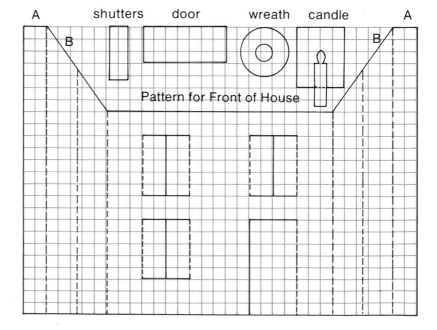

(1 square = ¼ inch)

110

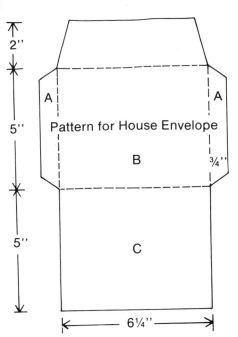

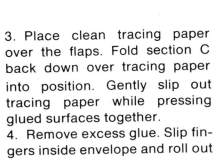

of liner. Check position and when dry, press surfaces together. Fold along dotted line so that liner bends over front of house like a roof.

6. Cut out dark green back and roof. Place house flat, face down as in Fig. 2. Be sure papers are even at bottom and sides. Glue dark green paper to entire back and roof, using tracing paper to position carefully. Green paper will be an eighth of an inch longer at the top. Trim along this edge with pinking shears to give roof a shingled effect. Fold the back down over front of house.

7. Cut out dark green shutters and door. Glue in position as shown by dotted lines in Fig. 1.

8. Cut out light green wreath. Use pinking shears to cut outer 1-inch circle. Fold in half and cut center circle with regular scissors in a zigzag fashion. (Pinking shears are too large to cut inner circle.) Glue wreath to door.

9. Write greeting on inside of roof.

10. Cut out envelope, using dimensions given in pattern.

11. See general instructions for assembling envelope.

Fig. 2

HOW TO ASSEMBLE ENVELOPES FOR HOUSE, SANTA AND CROWN

1. Copy pattern, following dimensions given, and cut out envelope. Cut on solid lines and fold on dotted lines.

2. Fold flaps marked A toward center of envelope. Slip tracing paper between flaps and section B to keep glue from adhering to section B. Apply glue to entire top of each flap A. Remove tracing paper. Quickly fold section C over onto flaps; press so glue transfers to section C. Lift up again and allow both surfaces to dry.

3. Place clean tracing paper over the flaps. Fold section C back down over tracing paper into position. Gently slip out tracing paper while pressing glued surfaces together.

4. Remove excess glue. Slip fingers inside envelope and roll out any excess glue.

5. Address envelope. Fold card flat and gently slip into envelope. Use a legal seal to close.

Santa

MATERIALS

red paper: 6x8 inches, plus 8½x 11½ inches for envelope
orange paper, 3x6 inches
white paper, 6x7 inches

DIRECTIONS

(For directions on how to enlarge a pattern, see p. 97.)
1. Copy patterns, enlarging as needed. Using pattern as a guide, cut out suit from red paper and fold along dotted line. Stand up like a tent.

(continued on next page)

Fig. 1

2. Cut out head from orange paper, snipping from A to nose, then carefully cutting along solid line for nose. Gently pull nose forward slightly. Punch out eyes with paper punch.

3. Apply glue to back of head below dotted line. (Do not apply glue to nose.) On red suit, apply glue to area below fold where head attaches (see Fig. 1). Let glue dry. Position the head so dotted line of head lines up with dotted line (or fold) of suit. Press to secure.

4. Cut out beard from white paper, using pinking shears to cut along curved lines. Fold along line A/B, bending semi-circle forward and down. Slip edge

A/B under nose as in Fig. 2. Fold lines A/E and B/F over edges of suit. Fold lines A/D and B/G in the opposite direction to inside of suit. Fold lines A/C and B/H over edges of

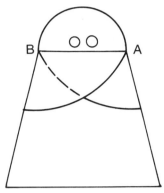

Fig. 3 (Back View)

back section of suit. Lines A/J and B/K should flap over each other in back, lining up with fold line A/B, as in Fig. 3.

5. Glue beard under nose in front along line A/B and in back along line A/B. Secure both flaps of beard to back of suit.

6. Cut out hat and fold along dotted line. Open and apply glue to inside. Let dry. Apply glue to both sides of head where hat attaches. Let dry. Carefully fold hat closed over head, as in

Fig. 4. Press firmly to secure.

7. To make the pompon for the hat, lightly glue two pieces of white paper together. Use pinking shears to cut pompon, then gently peel apart a portion of the two pieces of paper. Apply glue to point of hat on both sides; let dry. Position pompon and close paper over hat.

8. Cut out feet. Glue to inside of suit front. Gently fold along dotted lines so that feet lie flat.

9. Write a tiny greeting under mustache or on back of suit.

10. Cut out envelope, using dimensions given in pattern, and assemble. (General directions for assembling envelope follow directions for House.)

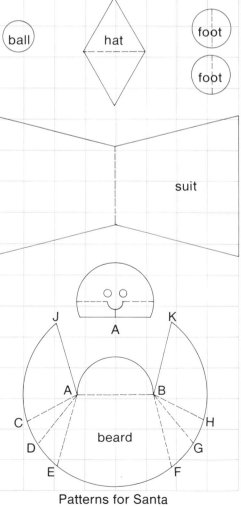

Patterns for Santa
(1 square = 1 square inch)

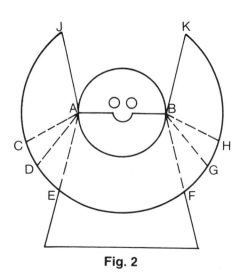

Fig. 2

Fig. 4

Crown

MATERIALS

pink paper, 4x13½ inches
orange paper: 2½x14 inches,
   plus 8½x11½ inches for the
   envelope

DIRECTIONS FOR CROWN

(For directions on how to enlarge a pattern, see p. 97.)
1. Copy patterns, enlarging as
needed. Using pattern A as a
guide, cut a strip of pink paper
4x13½ inches. Along the long
edge, mark off every 1⅛ inch,
then fold accordian fashion as
dotted lines indicate. Keep
folded and place flat, with first
fold on your right and cut edge
at left.

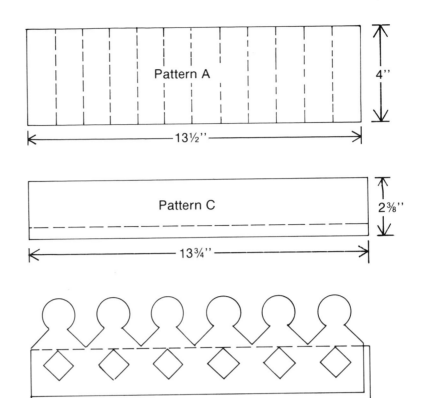

Fig. 1

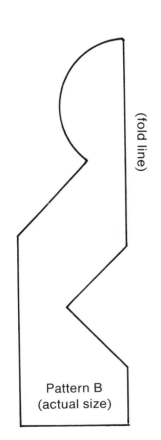

(fold line)

Pattern B
(actual size)

2. Cut out shape B from scrap
paper and place it directly on
top of folded strip, with longest
edge of B on the fold (or on the
right). Line up accurately and
trace design onto folded paper.
3. Cut out design with scissors
or X-acto knife. Cutting will be
easier if two or three folds are
cut at a time. Simply repeat the
pattern for the remaining folds.
4. When finished, gently bend
folds in opposite direction to
flatten paper neatly.
5. Using pattern C as a guide,
cut a strip of orange paper 2⅜x
13¾ inches. Draw a pencil
guideline ½ inch above bottom
edge as indicated by dotted line
in pattern C. Place pink paper
over orange paper along pencil
guideline as shown in Fig. 1.

Leave ¼ inch of orange strip extending beyond pink paper at
the right edge.
6. Glue in position, making sure
orange paper fills the diamond
cutouts of the pink paper.
7. Write a greeting on the inside
of the orange band. Bend the
crown into a circle, butting pink
edges together, with orange extension on the inside. Glue
neatly along this extension.
8. Cut out the envelope, using
dimensions given in pattern for
Santa, and assemble. (General
directions for assembling envelope follow directions for
House.)
9. Before slipping crown into
envelope, gently press it flat.

Bell

MATERIALS

purple paper, 7x11 inches
red paper, 9x9 inches

DIRECTIONS

(For directions on how to enlarge a pattern, see p. 97.)

1. Copy patterns, enlarging as
needed. Cut two bells from purple paper by folding paper and
placing dotted line of pattern on
fold.

2. Fold red paper and cut two
each of band A and band B. (Be
sure to place dotted line of B on
fold of paper.)

3. Place one bell flat (like an
open book), and glue red band
A to left half of ball, as in Fig. 1.
Glue red band B to right side,
placing cut edge in center of
bell and lining up folded edge of
B with outside edge of bell.
Wrap remainder of B around
back of bell on right and glue.

4. Place second bell flat and repeat Step 3 in opposite order.
(Glue band A to right side, and
band B to left side.)

5. From red paper, cut out card
9x5½ inches. (See card pattern.)
Fold line **a** so area **c** folds over
area **d.** Fold line **b** so area **e**
folds over area **c.** Open card
flat.

6. See Fig. 2. Glue entire left
half of first bell (A) to red card,
aligning fold of bell with fold **a** of
card. (Right half of bell will be
perpendicular to card.)

7. Glue the right half of the second bell (B) to red card, aligning
fold parallel to fold of first bell
and fold **a** of card.

8. From purple paper, cut
bands C and D. Glue in position,
as shown in Fig. 2. Trim any excess so edges of card are even.

9. Write greeting on D band and
fold. Close with legal seal.

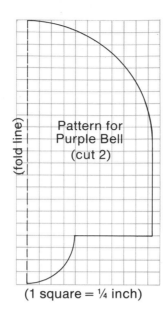

Pattern for Purple Bell (cut 2)

(fold line)

(1 square = ¼ inch)

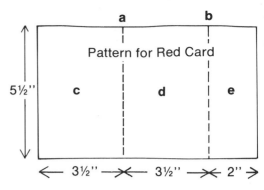

Pattern for Red Card

a   **b**

5½''

c   **d**   **e**

← 3½'' → ← 3½'' → ← 2'' →

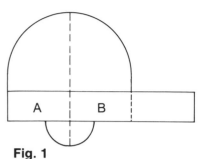

A   B

Fig. 1

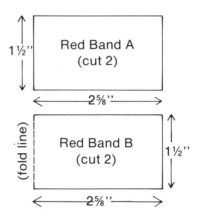

1½''

Red Band A (cut 2)

← 2⅝'' →

(fold line)

Red Band B (cut 2)

1½''

← 2⅝'' →

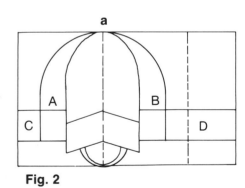

a

A   B

C   D

Fig. 2

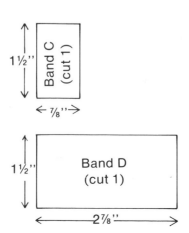

1½''

Band C (cut 1)

← ⅞'' →

1½''

Band D (cut 1)

← 2⅞'' →

Tree

MATERIALS

green paper, 7x12 inches
blue paper, 6x11 inches

DIRECTIONS

(For directions on how to enlarge a pattern, see p. 97.)
1. Enlarge tree pattern and label points A, B and C as shown.
2. Use pattern to copy the shape shown in Fig. 1 as follows: Position pattern as in section 1 on wrong side of green paper and trace, copying both solid and broken lines. Next, turn pattern over and position it to correspond with section 2; trace, copying solid and broken lines. Continue turning pattern and tracing to complete sections 3 and 4.

3. Cut out the design, cutting on solid lines only. This will be the tree.
4. Shape tree by folding paper on dotted line A/C; fold so that this line bends outward on the right side of the paper.
5. Next, fold on dotted lines marked A/B; fold so that crease bends inward on the right side of the paper. Finally, compress the tree on the folds; the shape should be a triangle the same size as tree pattern.
6. Place pattern on top of folded tree. Use paper punch to make holes where indicated. (Be careful not to punch through edges or folded edges.)
7. Using pattern, cut out a single triangle from blue paper. (Do not punch holes.) Glue this blue triangle between sections 2 and

3 of tree so that blue shows through the holes.
8. From blue paper, cut the card outline shown in Fig. 2 (a rectangle with a triangle at one end), using dimensions given. Do not mark the broken line on the blue paper. (Fig. 2 also shows assembled card; steps for assembling are given later.)
9. Fold the blue paper you have cut by taking edge F/G over to dotted line H/I to make a fold along D/E. Next, fold along H/I, bringing pointed end over to form a flap.
10. Open the blue paper and place tree inside, as shown in Fig. 2. The center fold of the tree should line up with fold D/E. Carefully glue outside edges of tree to blue paper. Close with legal seal.

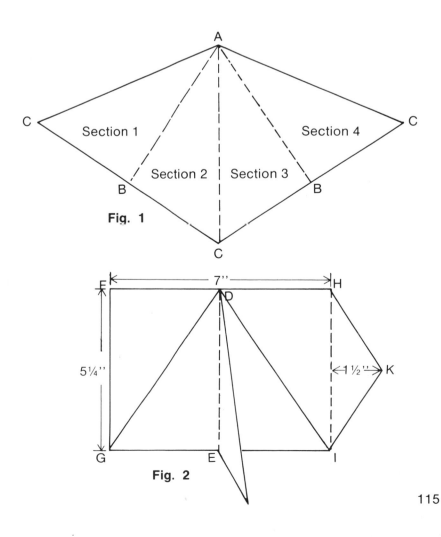

Pattern for Tree
(1 square = ¼ inch)

Fig. 1

Fig. 2

Picture-Perfect

(continued from p. 76)

a bulletin board of any size. Directions are given for the sample shown.

MATERIALS

1 wood-framed bulletin board, 17½x24 inches, and hangers
1 unfinished wood frame, rectangular, for 8x10-inch photo
1 unfinished wood frame, rectangular, for 4x5-inch photo
1 unfinished wood frame, rectangular, for 3x5-inch photo
4 wood rings (2 3-inch, 1 4-inch and 1 8-inch)
rub-on antique gold paint
craft glue
2 dozen fancy thumbtacks
photographs: 1 horizontal 8x10; 1 vertical 4x5; 1 horizontal 3x5; 2 to fit 3-inch circle; 1 to fit 4-inch circle; 1 to fit 8-inch circle

DIRECTIONS

1. Paint bulletin board frame and all photo frames and rings with gold paint. Allow to dry. Attach board's hangers to back. (If hangers are not sold with board, use 2 sawtooth hangers.)
2. Position all frames and rings on board as shown: with 8x10-inch frame in lower right corner, 4x5-inch frame in lower left corner, and 2 3-inch rings between these two; 8-inch ring in upper left corner, 3x5-inch frame in upper right corner, and 4-inch ring between these two.
3. Lift one frame at a time and spread glue on back. Replace in original position. Allow to dry.
4. Tack photos to board.

Note: If some materials are not available in your area, they may be ordered by mail. Two suppliers who stock macrame, decoupage and other craft supplies are: Merribee Needlearts and Crafts, P.O. Box 69, Fort Worth, Tex. 76101; and American Handicrafts Co., 1206 Walnut St., Philadelphia, Pa. 19107.

Baby Bib

(continued from p. 81)

top of the towel 4½ inches (including fringe) with right sides together and place half-circle pattern on the fold so that it is centered between the sides of the towel. Cut out neckline.
2. Close the 15-inch length of ribbing to make a circle and join the cut ends, right sides together. Next, fold the 3-inch width in half, right sides out.
3. Use pins to divide the ribbing into 4 sections, placing a pin at the seam. Use pins to divide the neckline hole into 4 sections, placing a pin at center back.
4. Pin the 2 edges of the ribbing to the right side of the neckline. Begin by matching the seam on the ribbing to the center back of the neckline. Match the other pin markings (ribbing will be smaller than neckline).
5. Sew edges together with a zigzag stitch, stretching the ribbing to fit the neckline. (Do not stretch the terry cloth.) Press seam allowance down into bib.
6. Add an applique of your choice (we used a printed design cut from fabric). To attach, position design at center of bib. Attach with press-on bonding (cut the same shape as the design) or baste.
7. Sew applique to bib, using a close zigzag stitch on the machine. Clip threads; press.

Baby T-shirt

A touch of applique can turn a plain undershirt into something special to be worn with diapers, training pants, shorts or skirts.

MATERIALS

baby's undershirt
press-on interfacing
fabric scraps
press-on bonding fabric (optional)
baby rickrack (optional)
thread to coordinate with fabric scraps

DIRECTIONS

(For directions on how to enlarge a pattern, see p. 97.)
1. Prewash and dry shirt.
2. Press interfacing onto back of fabric scraps.
3. Enlarge applique patterns and transfer onto fabric scraps, or create your own applique designs, and cut out.
4. Center applique on front of undershirt. Place a piece of press-on bonding between shirt and applique to hold applique in place, or baste.
5. Adjust sewing machine to do best possible satin stitch, with width on widest zigzag pattern. Satin-stitch applique to shirt.
6. Set sewing machine on a decorative pattern and stitch around the neckline "shoulder flaps"; then stitch around the sleeves along reinforced arm seams. If your machine has no decorative stitch patterns, apply baby rickrack.
7. Hem sleeves and bottom of shirt with a lingerie stitch or with a zigzag stitch set at medium width and length.
8. Clip threads and press shirt.

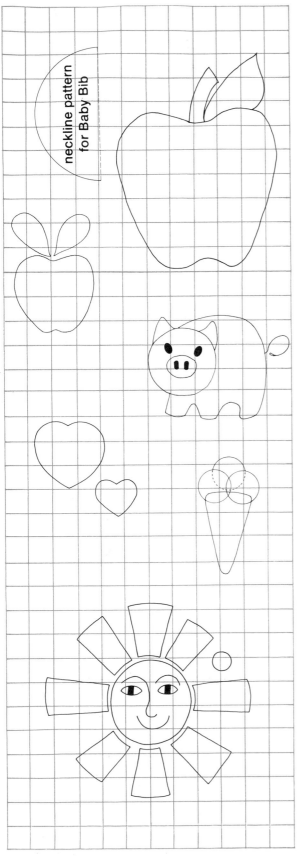

(1 square = 1 square inch)

Orange Flower

(continued from p. 83)

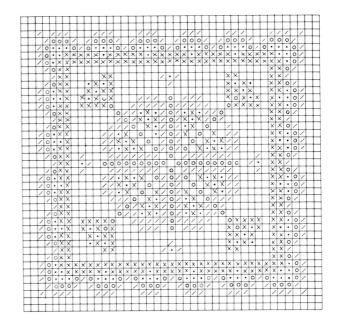

MATERIALS

7-mesh Penelope canvas, 16½ inches square
masking tape (optional)
wool tapestry yarn: 3 oz. rust; 1 oz. yellow; 1 oz. gold; 1 oz. orange; 1 oz. peach
tapestry needle or yarn needle with blunt point
backing fabric, 15½ inches square (preferably narrow-wale or no-wale corduroy)
thread to match
polyester fiberfill

COLOR CODE

☐ rust
● yellow
x gold
/ orange
o peach

Stripe

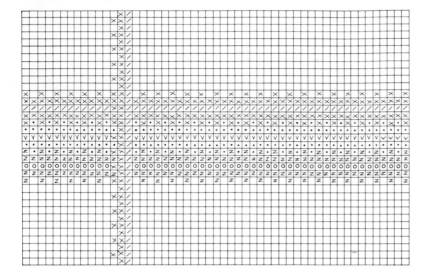

MATERIALS

7-mesh Penelope canvas,
   14½x20½ inches
masking tape (optional)
wool tapestry yarn: 4 oz. white; 1
   oz. brown; ½ oz. oatmeal; 1
   oz. henna; ½ oz. peach; 1 oz.
   gold; ½ oz. yellow
tapestry needle or yarn needle
   with blunt point
backing fabric, 13½x19½ inches
   (preferably narrow-wale or
   no-wale corduroy); thread to
   match
polyester fiberfill

COLOR CODE

☐ white
x brown
/ oatmeal
● henna
v peach
z gold
o yellow

Blue Snowflake

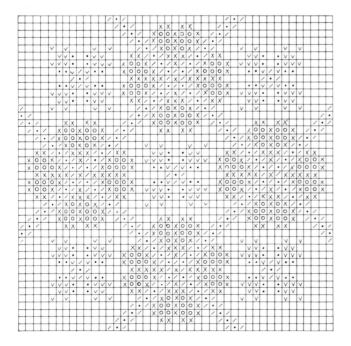

MATERIALS

7-mesh Penelope canvas, 17½
   inches square
masking tape (optional)
wool tapestry yarn: 3 oz. white;
   1½ oz. cobalt blue; ½ oz. pewter; 1 oz. lime; 1 oz. emerald; 1
   oz. light blue
tapestry needle or yarn needle
   with blunt point
backing fabric, 16½ inches
   square (preferably narrow-
   wale or no-wale corduroy);
   thread to match
polyester fiberfill

COLOR CODE

☐ white
x cobalt
o pewter
● lime
/ emerald
v light blue

118

Linda

(continued from p. 85)

ing. Trim excess sock fabric. Repeat for second shoe top.

14. To make fronts of legs, machine-stitch each shoe top (C) to a leg piece. To make backs of legs, machine-stitch each shoe bottom (D) to a leg piece.

15. To complete each leg, pin a front to a back, right sides together; match seams where shoe joins leg. Machine-stitch up each side of leg, beginning at shoe seam.

16. Pin top and bottom of shoe together around toe curve; machine-stitch. Extra fabric on shoe bottom now falls into a fold that will form the heel. Pin raw edges of this fabric together and machine-stitch a curve to shape the heel (see dotted line on pattern). Trim seams to ⅛ inch.

17. Turn legs and shoes right side out. Stuff up to knees. Machine-stitch across top of knees as shown on pattern; then stuff rest of legs. Cut knee patches from dark pink felt and hand-stitch in place.

18. Slip each sock cuff into position and hand-stitch cut edge along top of shoe. Cuff will go up leg.

19. Cut 2 strips of black vinyl, ½x2¼ inches, for shoe straps. Turn edges under ⅛ inch and machine-stitch. Hand-stitch the straps and buttons to shoes.

20. Pin legs in open seam of body; close seam with hand-stitching.

21. Hand-stitch arms to body.

22. Cut 4 collar pieces from white fabric. Place 2 pieces right sides together and machine-stitch, leaving back edge open. Turn right side out; close seam with hand-stitching. Repeat for other half of collar.

23. Cut 2 pieces of lace, each 7 inches long. Slightly gather lace and hand-stitch to underside of collar pieces along the edges. Join collar halves at front and back and hand-stitch around neck.

24. To make hair, loop 40 yards of rug yarn into 20-inch vertical loops. Place loops on a flat surface, keeping strands close together. (This should now measure about 5 inches across.) Place seam binding horizontally across yarn loops where the center "part" will be. Machine-stitch through seam binding and yarn. Pin hair into position and hand-stitch seam binding to head. Gather yarn into pigtails; tie with ribbon. Trim yarn ends.

25. Turn bottom edge of skirt under ⅛ inch. Machine-stitch lace to this edge. Gather top edge to fit waist and hand-stitch to body.

26. Attach buttons to dress.

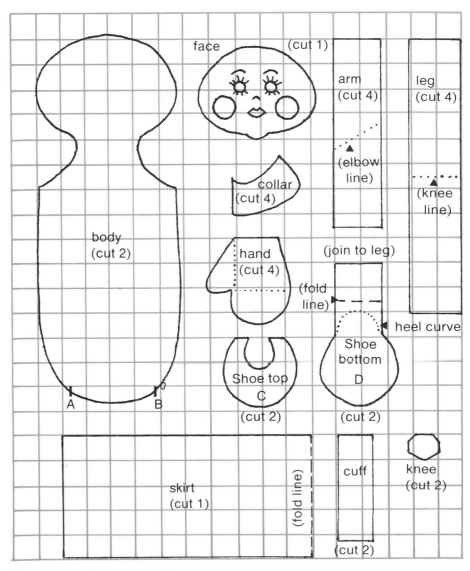

face (cut 1)
arm (cut 4)
leg (cut 4)
(elbow line)
(knee line)
collar (cut 4)
body (cut 2)
hand (cut 4)
(join to leg)
(fold line)
heel curve
Shoe bottom D
Shoe top C
(cut 2)
(cut 2)
A
B
skirt (cut 1)
(fold line)
cuff (cut 2)
knee (cut 2)

(1 square = 1 square inch)

119

Nativity

(continued from p. 88)

(1 square = 1 square inch)

Tree

Ornaments

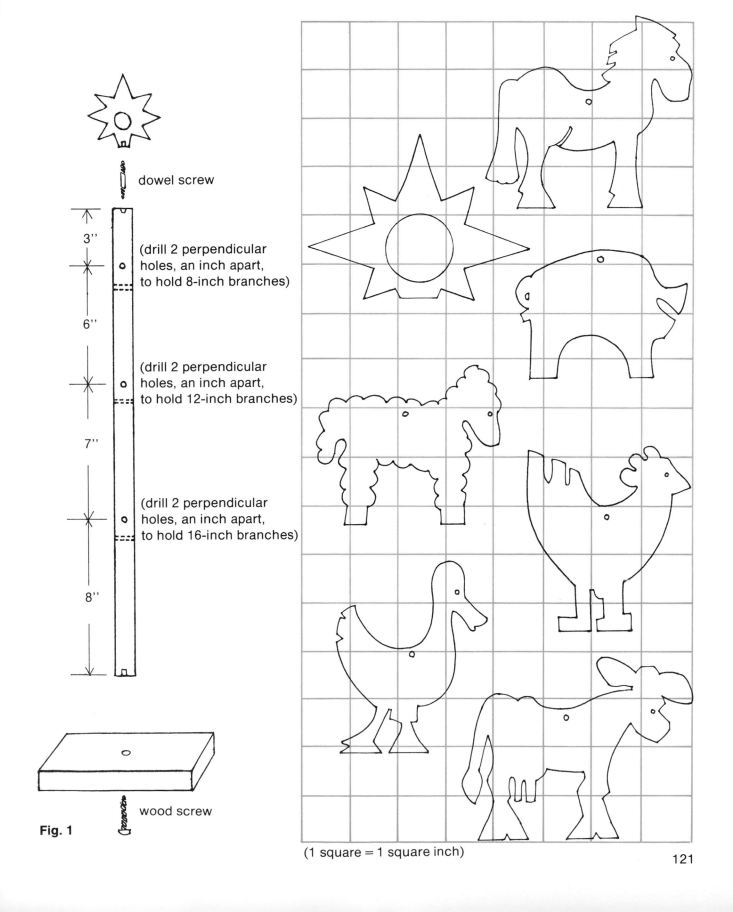

dowel screw

3''

(drill 2 perpendicular holes, an inch apart, to hold 8-inch branches)

6''

(drill 2 perpendicular holes, an inch apart, to hold 12-inch branches)

7''

(drill 2 perpendicular holes, an inch apart, to hold 16-inch branches)

8''

wood screw

Fig. 1

(1 square = 1 square inch)

Critters

(continued from p. 87)

Patterns for Cat

Patterns for Bunny

Patterns for Mouse

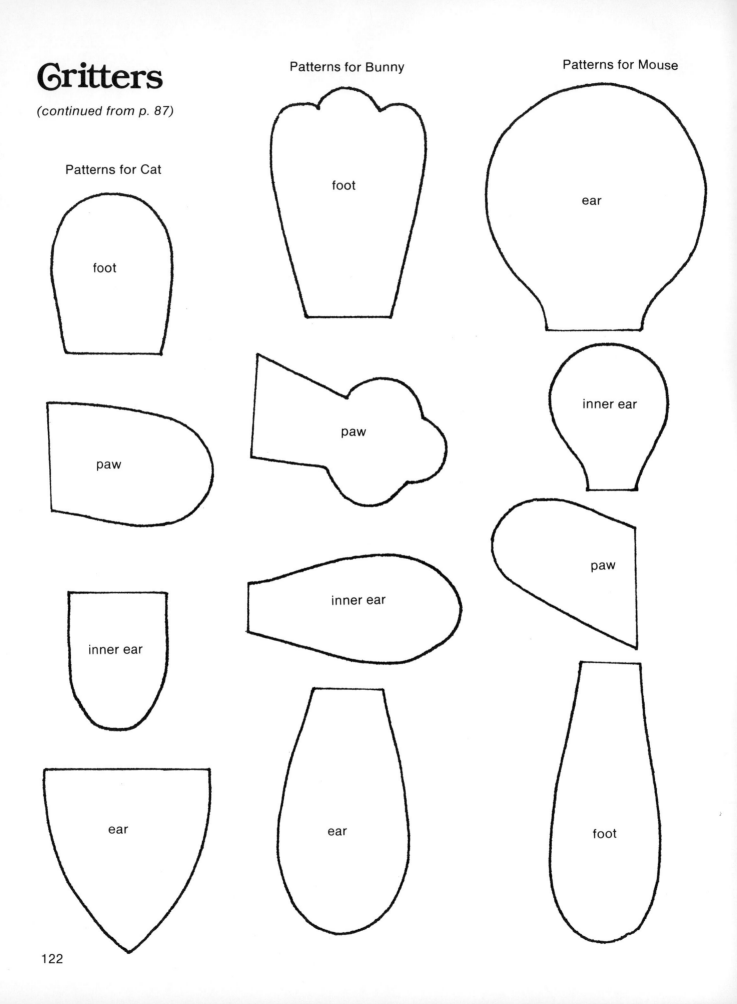

foot

foot

ear

paw

paw

inner ear

inner ear

inner ear

paw

ear

ear

foot

Index

RECIPES

beverages
Fluffy Orange Nog, 14

breads and pastries
Banana Tea Bread, 29
Christmas Coffee Ring, 20
Christmas Eve Saffron
  Braid, 18
Christmas Fruit-Nut Loaf, 28
Christmas Morning
  Brioche, 20
Finnish Coffee Braid, 18
Golden Parmesan Rolls, 9
Lefse I, 12-13
Lefse II, 13
Lefse III, 13
Miniature Cheesecake
  Jewels, 15
Orange Bread, 29
Orange Swirl Buns, 29
Pumpkin Date Bread, 29
Regal Savarin Ring, 20
Sugared Yeast
  Doughnuts, 30

candies and confections
Almond-Studded Logs, 27
Buttery Almond Brittle, 27
Candied Fruit Squares, 26
Caramel Nut Logs, 27
Crystal Mint Drops, 27
Deluxe Peanut Butter
  Fudge, 27
Fondant, 26
Fondant Balls, 27
New Orleans Pralines, 28
Pastel Mint Patties, 27
Peppermint Pinwheel
  Patties, 26
Stuffed Dates, 26
Stuffed Pecan Halves, 27

cheeses
Bacon-Cheddar Fondue, 21
Blue Cheese Ball, 23
Cheddar Cheese Ball, 23
Clam Cheese Fondue, 23
Double Cheese Fondue, 21
Golden Pizza Fondue, 21
Salmon-Pecan Ball, 23

cookies
Almond-Raspberry Bars, 24
Candied Fruit Bars, 25
Christmas Jewels, 24
Hand-painted Butter
  Cookies, 24
Jumbo Oatmeal-Peanut
  Butter Cookies, 25

desserts
Holiday Trifle, 17
Miniature Cheesecake
  Jewels, 15

dressings
Range Top Pecan, 8

fillings and frostings
Almond Glaze, 18
Honey Filling, 20
Orange Frosting, 25
Vanilla Glaze, 20
Vanilla Icing, 25

jams and jellies
Cranberry-Banana
  Conserve, 30
Easy Apple Jelly, 30

relishes and condiments
Cranberry Blender
  Relish, 11
Mixed-Vegetable
  Marinade, 15

salads
Cranberry Blender
  Relish, 11
Cranberry-Marshmallow
  Cream, 11
Cranberry-Orange Ring, 11
Shimmering Apple Mold, 17
Two-Layer Cranberry-
  Cream Cheese Mold, 11

salad dressings
Whipped Dressing, 11

sauces
Custard, 17
Raspberry, 17

snacks
Creamy Tuna Spread, 14

stews
Meatball and Bean, 15
Oyster Stew I, 7
Oyster Stew II, 7
Oyster Stew III, 7

vegetables
Au Gratin Potato Bake, 17
Butternut Squash with
  Peas, 9
Creamy Mashed Potatoes, 8

CRAFTS

angels
clothespin, 70-71; 109
cornhusk, 67-69
felt, 45

animal ornaments
of calico, 86-87; 122
of felt, 59-60; 90-91
of wood, 39-40; 88-89

applique, 80-81; 116-117

arrangements, dried, 62-64

Baby Bib, 80-81; 116-117

Baby T-Shirt, 116-117

banners, 54-56; patterns for,
  103-105

baskets, 54, 57

calico
Critters, 86-87; 122
ornaments of, 47-49

cards, Christmas, 72-73;
  110-115

centerpiece, dried, 62; 64

childproof decorations,
  88-89

children, enjoying Christmas
  with, 93-94

Christmas in the Country, 2

Christmas Story, 4-5; pattern
  for crewel, 99-101

Christmas tree. See tree.

clothespin crafts, 70-71; 109

cornhusk craft, 67-69;
  108-109

dolls
clothespin, 70-71
cornhusk, 67-69; 108
Long-legged Linda, 84-85;
  119

Double Cross-Stitch Pillows,
  82-83; 117-118

dried plant arrangements,
  62-64

duffel bag, 79

felt
ornaments of, 41-46; 59-61;
  patterns for, 106-107
stockings, 42-44
tree, 58-61

garment bag, 78

gifts
for children to make, 94
choosing the perfect, 95-96
wrappings for, 31-33

invitations, 76-77

Keepsake Clock, 75-76

lace, ornaments of, 50-51

Long-legged Linda, 84-85;
  119

Love banner, 54-56; 104

Luke, Gospel according to,
  4-5

Mouse House, 90-92

napkin rings, Poinsettia, 66;
  108

Nativity, wooden, 88

ornaments
of calico, 47-49
for children to make, 93
of felt, 41-46; 59-61
of lace, 50-51
of wood, 38-40; 89

photos, frames for, 74-76; 116

pillows, Double Cross-Stitch,
  82-83; 117-118

rubber cement, tips for using,
  110

Santa
Christmas card, 111-112
clothespin, 71; 109
felt, 45
gift wrap, 32

shirts, 80-81; 116-117

Slumber Shirt, 80-81; 117

soldier
banner, 54-55
clothespin, 71

stockings, Christmas, 42-44

Sunshine Shirt, 80-81; 117

tablecloth, Pine Tree, 64-66

Three Kings Banner, 54-56;
  105

threshold decorations, 53;
  102

tree
Christmas card, 115
dried weed, 64
felt, 58-61; 106-107
gift wrap, 32
live, 34-37
picking the perfect, 37
wooden, 88-89; 120

wood
cutouts, 38-40
Nativity, 88; 121
shavings, 38-39
tree and ornaments for,
  88-89; 120

wreath
dried herb, 64
Mug of Good Wishes, 53;
  102
Skater's, 53; 102

CREDITS

INTRODUCTION—p. 3: photo by Grant Heilman; pp. 4-5: design by Maureen Sweeney; crewel work by Elizabeth Bradley; photo by Fred Carbone.

CHAPTER 1—pp. 6, 9, 10 and 12: photos by William Hazzard/ Hazzard Studios.

CHAPTER 2—p. 15: photo by William Hazzard/Hazzard Studios; p. 16: top left photo by Al J. Reagan; top right and bottom photos by William Hazzard/Hazzard Studios; bottom photo by Al J. Reagan; pp. 22, 25 and 26: photos by William Hazzard/Hazzard Studios; p. 31: designs by Maureen Sweeney; photo by Meillier/ McCune.

CHAPTER 3—p. 35: top photo courtesy National Christmas Tree Association; bottom photos, from left: Gloria McNutt, Gloria McNutt, Fred Carbone; p. 37: illlustrations courtesy USDA; p. 38: top and bottom left, design and photos by Gloria McNutt; bottom right, designs by Gretchen Bathgate; photo by Fred Carbone; p. 41: designs and photos by Gloria McNutt; p. 47: designs by Bonnie Sargent; photos by Fred Carbone; p. 51: designs by Jean Gillies; photos by Hoedt Studios.

CHAPTER 4—p. 53: designs by Janet DeBard; crafts by Marie Schulz; photos by Susan Dooley; p. 58: banner designs and photos by Gloria McNutt; basket designs by Janet DeBard; basket photo by Susan Dooley; p. 57: designs by Janet DeBard; photo by Susan Dooley; p. 58: designs by Irene Laverty; photos by Fred Carbone; p. 60: designs by Mrs. Richard Myers; photos by Jay Paris; pp. 64-66: tablecloth designs by Jessie MacDonald; napkin ring designs by Marion Schafer; p. 67: designs by Linda Horn; photos by Fred Carbone; p. 70: designs by Maureen Sweeney; photo by Fred Carbone.

CHAPTER 5—p. 73: designs by Bonnie Sargent; photo by Michael Durning; p. 74: designs by Linda Kauss; photos by Daniel R. Milburn; p. 79: designs by Clara Rose Thomas; photo by Fred Carbone; p. 80: designs by Sunshine Company; photos by Fred Carbone; p. 83: designs by Janet Mysse/Janknits; photo by Fred Carbone.

CHAPTER 6—p. 85: design and photo by Gloria McNutt; p. 86: designs by Sunshine Company; photo by Fred Carbone; p. 89: designs by Rosalie Waranius Vass; photos by Fred Carbone; p. 90: designs by Bonnie Sargent; photo by Fred Carbone.